Reading
STEPHEN
KING

Reading STEPHEN KING

Edited by
Brian James Freeman

CEMETERY DANCE PUBLICATIONS • 2023

Reading Stephen King
Copyright © 2017 by Brian James Freeman

Cover Design © 2023 by Desert Isle Design, LLC
Interior Design © 2023 by Desert Isle Design, LLC

All rights reserved. No part of this book may be reproduced in any form or by any electronic or mechanical means, including information storage and retrieval systems, without permission in writing from the publisher, except by a reviewer who may quote brief passages in a review.

Trade Paperback Edition

ISBN:
978-1-58767-942-1

This book is a work of fiction. Names, characters, places and incidents either are products of the author's imagination or are used fictitiously. Any resemblance to actual events or locales or persons, living or dead, is entirely coincidental.

Cemetery Dance Publications
132B Industry Lane, Unit #7
Forest Hill, MD 21050
www.cemeterydance.com

TABLE OF CONTENTS

7	Sometimes You Go Back	— Stewart O'Nan
13	Afterword for the 30th Anniversary Edition of *Christine*
	—Richard Chizmar
17	Introduction to *Knowing Darkness: Artists Inspired by Stephen King* — Frank Darabont
29	Spock's Not the Only One Who Can Mind Meld: Stephen King and the Telepathy of Writing — Stephen Spignesi
45	Disappearing Down That Rabbit Hole — Justin Brooks
59	The Politics of Being Stephen King — Tony Magistrale
73	The Adventure of Reading Stephen King — Michael R. Collings
89	Reading the Lost Works of Stephen King — Rocky Wood
109	Twins and Twinning in Stephen King's Dark Tower Novels — Robin Furth
155	King Since Scribner — Kevin Quigley
155	Being a Non-US Stephen King Fan — Hans-Åke Lilja
165	The Role of God in Stephen King's Desperation — Billy Chizmar
181	*From a Buick 8* by Stephen King: A Review — Jack Ketchum
189	Living in a Web of Mystery — Bev Vincent
201	The One That Got Away — Mick Garris
209	My Accidental Obsession with Stephen King — Jay Franco
217	Stephen King Celebration — Clive Barker

Sometimes You Go Back

◆

STEWART O'NAN

I like the old ones. The elder gods, as H.P. used to say. The elementals. *'Salem's Lot. The Shining. Night Shift. The Stand.* There's that sweet spot he hit right at the beginning, but also, this is when I first started reading him. Everything from *Carrie* all the way through *Pet Sematary*—those are the ones I go back to over and over like touchstones. I must own a half dozen copies of *Different Seasons*, and every time I'm in Half Price Books I look for more. I still need the tangerine one to complete the set.

It's generational, I think. You love the books of his you started with, wherever you got on the merry-go-round. For readers one generation younger than me, the big book is *It*. I like *It* (like *It*, like *It*, yes I do), but I can go six or seven years before I have to go back to the standpipe and the library and walk over that bridge again.

As Ben and Bev and Eddie will tell you, it's different going back. Pennywise is twenty-eight now—eternal, sure, pure evil, but we've known him a good long time. Maybe not a neighbor, but he's part of Derry the way Sheriff Bannerman will always be part of Castle Rock. Yes, he's lurking in the sewers, which is still unnerving, but he can't terrify us the way he did when we first met.

Talking of watching horror movies a second or third or tenth time, the man himself says we're not so much being scared as recalling the memory of being scared, and how thrilling it was, how fun. There's a familiarity that's comforting as Michael Myers stalks Laurie Strode down the leafy streets of Haddonfield or the Thing's thrashing tentacles lash the Antarctic air. No matter how we try, we can't un-see what we've already seen, un-know what we already know (Rumsfeld excluded). You can't go home again, and yet, as a reader, I find I'm always trying to recreate that first time, those virgin nights as a teenager I stayed up till three following Tom Cullen through the Mormon Mountains, when who strangled those poor girls in Castle Rock was a mystery. I want to have the undiscovered country of those books sprawling out in front of me like the desert the dark man flees across at the beginning of *The Gunslinger*, when anything might happen.

Impossible, yet I still try. My tactics are simple. Like a primitive, I use sympathetic magic, restaging, as in a ritual, the original experience. If I'm re-reading *The Dead Zone*, I'll pull out my old Signet paperback from 1980, E9338, the glossy black binding chipped and fissured white, the pages gone brown and brittle at the edges, smelling of dust and mildew. The cover reminds me, pointlessly, that it was a #1 bestseller the year I graduated from high school. The price of $3.50 recalls the wire carousel bookracks drugstores and bus stations used to have, when cheap, handy mass-market paperbacks ruled.

Sometimes You Go Back

It's nostalgic, this wish to go back to the perfect past, return to a world you've loved and lost. Terrible things will happen to Johnny Smith, you know, but all of your favorite characters are there, even the hateful Greg Stillson, and all your favorite scenes, those moments you can still summon up from the last time you read the book. There will be little things you don't remember, those tasty tidbits he's so good at—the movie house is The Shade—but mostly you know the way, and the major landmarks. Sarah and the carnival midway. The crash. Frank Dodd dead on the toilet with the lipsticked sign around his neck: I CONFESS. You know where you're going to end up and lean forward, anticipating those big climaxes—which is not at all how the book worked your first time through. Then it was all suspense, the set-up and build-up was torturous, exquisite, naturally blooming into the surprise and satisfaction of the payoff, the master's forte. Now you know as well as Johnny what awaits him. Unlike him, you don't dread it. No, in fact you're even more impatient to get there. You have to slow yourself down, take pleasure in noticing the subtle touches, the ironic asides, the details which at the time were utterly contemporary and widely shared, the roadside detritus of daily American life, but now belong like curios to that weird post-Vietnam/Watergate era. So it's not just the larger plot effects but the small stuff and the overall pacing that's changed.

And there's the whole problem now of reading it like a writer—the very writing that inspired you to become one—pulling a scene or a section apart to see what he's doing, how he's using delay to create suspense or characterizing someone through dialogue. You stop to marvel or just appreciate a smart choice and the dream turns into words on a page, spaces and punctuation, and you're no longer in Otisfield with the two grab-assing kids who find Carol Dunbarger's bare foot sticking out of the snow. You're in your chair in your room and have to relax and conjure that world so you can drop into it again.

It's easy, though, because it's all there, as real as the house you grew up in, or the streets of your old neighborhood, overlaid with images of Christopher Walken and Martin Sheen from the Cronenberg version you haven't seen in a decade, and the memory of the last time you read it, on a sagging bunk bed in a cabin, with a lake breeze and the shouts of children playing freeze tag pouring through a rusty screen. The layers are at once delicious and distracting, a kind of time machine. You're happy to be back there, except you're not really there, you're from the future, just visiting, but for a couple hundred pages you can pretend it's the past and everything's still ahead of you.

Johnny knows what you're going through. In the end, in the farewell letter he leaves behind, he tells Sarah it's sometimes hard to believe there was such a year as 1970, and that at others it's a handsbreadth away.

A handsbreadth. Yes, exactly.

The Dead Zone, like "The Body," closes with a bittersweet nod to the mystery of Time and Change—Fortune, really. Fate. It's true, the middle-aged you thinks as you peruse the lists of other bestselling Signet titles you might enjoy that fill the endpages (prices slightly higher in Canada)—*Sins of Omission* by Chelsea Quinn Yarbro, *Savage Ransom* by David Lippincott—consigned now to the bargain bins of history, re-read by no one. What is the lesson here? *Nothing is ever lost*, Johnny says, yet so little seems to last, and as you close the book, you think, at least there's this, and reverently set it on the shelf again with the others, knowing eventually you'll be back, grateful that they'll always be there waiting for you, knowing, even as you've been reading, he's making more.

Afterword for the 30th Anniversary Edition of *Christine*

RICHARD CHIZMAR

Like many longtime readers, I can chart the course of my life by when and where I read most of Stephen King's books. *Bag of Bones* was sitting by a friend's hospital bed every day for a week. *Insomnia* while lying in a hospital bed myself. *Black House* in a three-day frenzy at the beach after a surprise phone call from Akiva Goldsman asking me to help adapt the novel into a screenplay. And *It*, as a college junior, the week after I walked away from a collegiate lacrosse career that I believed at the time defined me as a human being. In that regard, *It* may have just saved the life of a very lost and very confused young man. At the very least, it carved the path for my writing and editing career and gave me something to dream about again.

Pretty much all of Steve's books are like that for me. Personal. Meaningful. Special. Most of the early ones seemed to magically come along at just the right time for me. I've listened to many other readers, writers, and editors tell me the same thing about Steve's books and their own lives.

And then there is *Christine*...

RICHARD CHIZMAR

Originally published in hardcover in the spring of 1983, I was just about to graduate from high school and my world consisted of sports, girls, and friends. Not necessarily in that order.

In other words, I was the exact same age as Arnie, Dennis, and Leigh, the main characters of the novel. I was closer to Dennis than Arnie, thanks to my position on a State Championship lacrosse team, but there was plenty of Arnie in me, too. I never went anywhere without a book in my hand or backpack. I was a pretty quiet guy. I liked girls, but was usually shy around them. I didn't suffer from acne as Arnie did, thank God, and I didn't share his passion for old cars, despite the fact that my father practically lived in the garage tinkering with our family cars. But my point is...I knew these three characters. Just as I knew the Buddy Reppertons of the school and neighborhood. Intimately. Parts of them were either inside myself, or inside the friends and classmates I walked the halls with each and every day at Edgewood High School.

I remember reading *Christine* over the course of about two weeks. Not real fast, but as I mentioned earlier, I was pretty busy with sports and friends and girls. I remember loving the book, being scared by the book, and most of all feeling sad because of the book. Why? Because there was so much *truth* in the book.

I think that's the main reason why most of Steve's stories are so memorable. Whether it's a flat-out scare-the-shit-outta-you horror story (*Carrie*, *'Salem's Lot*, *The Shining*) or a story that tiptoes more on the mainstream ("The Body," "Rita Hayworth and Shawshank Redemption," *The Green Mile)*, there is always *truth* inside his words and characters. That's why they *live*.

Afterword for the 30th Anniversary Edition of *Christine*

For me, *Christine* is probably the most melancholy of all of Steve's novels, especially those last 50 pages or so (with *The Dead Zone* and a couple others nipping right at its heels). Sure, for some people, it's about a haunted car and a loser and his controlling mom and pretty girlfriend. But for me, it's a story about growing up and how you do it alone no matter how close you are to your parents and your best friend, and a story about letting go...of your youth and innocence, the pedestal some of us—if we are lucky—put our parents upon, and maybe hardest of all, letting go of some of our friendships that we believed would last forever. I know that is what reached the deepest inside me at the time. You see, I had best friends like Arnie in my own life at age 17, and it was just occurring to me—even as I was reading Steve's novel—that as each day of that spring was passing, those friends and I were growing further and further apart. And there was nothing I could do to stop it from happening. It was...*life*.

There is a passage very late in the book that I can remember exactly where I was sitting when I first read it. It broke my heart then, and it breaks my heart now.

> So that's my story. Except for the dreams.
> I'm four years older, and Arnie's face has grown hazy to me, a browning photograph from an old yearbook. I never would have believed that could happen, but it has. I made it through, made the transition from adolescence to manhood—whatever that is—somehow; I've got a college degree on which the ink is almost dry, and I've been teaching junior high history. I started last year, and two of my original

students—Buddy Repperton types, both of them—were older than I was. I'm single, but there are a few interesting ladies in my life, and I hardly ever think of Arnie at all.

Except in the dreams.

It broke my heart because it was going to happen to me, too. It already was. And, man, it hurt.

I look back now, some 30 years later, and I can remember their names. The friends of my childhood. Some I still see on a regular basis, and I am beyond grateful for that. Some are the occasional text or email. Some are no longer living. And some of their faces are lost to me forever, just as Arnie's face was lost to Dennis.

But you know what? I can still see and hear and feel Arnie and Dennis and Leigh. Right now today. Right here today. That is the gift of a special story. That is the *magic* of a special story.

I'm grateful to Steve for writing *Christine* and to Pete Crowther for asking me to write this Afterword. It hurt to remember. And it hurt a little to write this. But it was worth it.

Introduction to *Knowing Darkness: Artists Inspired by Stephen King*

FRANK DARABONT

Let's talk *love*:

I love art. I'm an absolute nut for it. To me, what a skilled artist does is a magic trick. It's alchemy. It's a talent I lack but greatly admire, which is why I'm so impressed by those who do it. These magicians put lines on paper or canvas, and at some point the alchemy occurs: the lines cease to be just lines and something *else* happens. Something springs to life. A character is created. A story is told. There's depth and mood and tone and meaning—or at the very least, something that looks like what it's supposed to be.

I'm a hardcore fan of old-school illustrative art, and I mean "old-school" as a high compliment. It's the sort of art embodied in this stunning book. It's art in the tradition of Norman Rockwell, Joseph Leyendecker, N.C. Wyeth, and Maxfield Parrish. Those are the name-brand heavyweights, of course, but let's also acknowledge and admire the work done by all the countless artists—often unheralded and laboring in obscurity—who've graced our lives and imaginations for generations going back to the popular mass periodicals of the

19th century. They are the people who chose illustration as a calling, rolled up their sleeves, and worked on deadlines to put food on the table. There are high-falutin' exceptions, of course (Claude Monet blows my mind *big-time*, for example), but generally the work that tugs at my heart the most is the stuff I grew up with and which highbrow critics have always tended to dismiss: comic book art, paintings for movie posters, book cover art, that sort of thing.

You'd know my tastes if you saw my house—not to brag, but I have a pretty swell collection of original art here. My Bernie Wrightson comic book covers and splash pages make me swoon. My Drew Struzan movie poster paintings make me giddy. My Mike Mignola *Hellboy* paintings give me joy. As I sit and write this, Stephen King himself peers over my shoulder from the wonderful 1991 cover painting David Voigt did for *Cinefantastique* magazine, wherein our favorite bestselling author seems smugly unaware that a sledgehammer-wielding Kathy Bates is lurking behind him (or maybe he's looking smug because he *damn well knows* she's there, and he *can't wait* to see the looks on our faces when she abruptly flips out and sends his brains flying toward us). You'll find these pieces of art throughout my home alongside works by Bob Peak, Bill Stout, Sanjulian, Graham Ingels, Eric Powell, and a variety of others. I love each and every one of them. I pass them in their frames and consider myself a lucky man. I never let a day go by—even the hurried and stressful days—without pausing to soak some of it in and admire the work of one or another of those artists.

Stephen King loves art too. He *gets* it. He *digs* it. You can tell, because the art that graces his books is never an afterthought. It is *important* to him. And because it's important

Introduction to *Knowing Darkness: Artists Inspired by Stephen King*

to him, it tends to have tremendous impact on us—it does, at times, have the ability to dazzle. I'd say the jewel in the crown would have to be the body of artwork that graces his literary magnum opus, The Dark Tower series. The illustrations spanning those books are as epic as the books themselves. The seven volumes were rendered by six different artists with *very* different styles, but there's a deeply pleasing cohesion to it all—no surprise, I suppose, because the artists were all drawing their water from the well of Steve King's imagination.

And it's quite a well, that well of Steve's. God knows how deep it goes. The water it offers up is at times brackish and tainted, sometimes gruesome and foul, sometimes sweeter than the milk of human kindness itself. It can kill you dead as Caesar in the most appalling ways imaginable or resurrect you like Lazarus and lift your soul to heaven. As tools go, Steve's imagination is as potent as a nuke. He's been delivering the goods to his readers for going on *four decades* now, and just when you think he must be close to using up all the water in his well, he'll just dig the darn thing deeper and surprise us all over again.

In short, he's one hell of a resource if you're an illustrative artist looking to get inspired. Not only is he the most vivid and visual of writers, but there is no end to the subject matter from which to draw—how many characters, how many events, how many "other worlds than these" are on offer? Take your pick and break out your brushes.

I love Stephen King. As a storyteller, as a man, as a friend. Let me tell you a little something about him:

From a fan letter I wrote to Steve when I was 21 years old has sprung a friendship that is now almost three decades along (I just turned 50 a few months ago as I write this—holy shit, folks!). It is a friendship that has done what the best ones do: given me delight and comfort through the years. As a person, he is one of the most open-minded, down-to-earth, and loyal people it's ever been my pleasure and good fortune to know. More than anything, Steve is defined by a level of sheer *generosity* that is inspiring and humbling. I could write reams about his decency alone. If God is ever looking for that one righteous man, I say look no further than Steve King.

From the tiny seed of that letter I wrote to him in 1980 has also grown a professional relationship that has enriched us both on many levels beyond the merely monetary. For my part, it is not overstating it to say that he has been a patron saint to my filmmaking career. I am a director today because of Steve, who has to date entrusted four of his wonderful stories to my care. One of them, "Rita Hayworth and Shawshank Redemption," from the *Different Seasons* collection, provided me my break into feature film directing... never an easy break to get in Hollywood, but made possible in that case solely on the strength of Steve's story.

He is also a publishing phenomenon, and has been since 1973 when his first novel, *Carrie*—a small book with big ideas—saw print and became a surprise bestseller. His second novel in 1975, *'Salem's Lot,* built on that success. I myself was slow to catch on and didn't discover Stephen King until his *third* book was published in 1977. It fell into my hands purely by accident...or possibly by divine providence. You decide:

I was a senior in high school—Jimmy Carter was president, disco ruled (you couldn't escape it), and I had joined a book-of-the-month club called The Literary Guild because their come-on was too tempting to resist: I got to order a

Introduction to *Knowing Darkness: Artists Inspired by Stephen King*

stack of hardcover books for a dime, after which I was committed to buy a certain number of books at their regular book-club prices. Every month they'd send me a pamphlet describing the upcoming monthly selection—the trick being that if I *didn't* want that book shipped to me automatically, I had to remember to send the little card back to them.

I seldom had the money as a teenager for the wild luxury of a new book, even at low book club cost, so I almost always sent the card back. But every so often I'd be scatterbrained and forget to do it, and a book I hadn't meant to order would arrive in the mail. Cursing myself, I'd open the package long enough to pull the book out and glance at the cover—but lacking the funds to buy, I'd inevitably repackage the book and ship it back unread...

...with one notable exception. My memory of this is quite vivid. On this one occasion, when I pulled the book I hadn't meant to order from its box, I found myself holding a novel called *The Shining* by some guy named Stephen King. (His name didn't really ring a bell despite my having seen and loved the movie *Carrie* a few years before.) I couldn't tell much about the book, except that it had pretty cool cover... an intriguing cover...a *spooky* cover.

Well, "spooky" is right up my alley. The cover art montage by Dave Christensen depicted an old Victorian building, an adult couple, some ominous-looking hedge animals, a long wooden mallet, and a little boy staring at us with blank whites where his eyeballs should have been. The art made great use of negative space as it wrapped around the spine, drifting off into a snowy void on the back of the book.

It was the boy's blank white eyes, more than anything, that did it...that small, almost unobtrusive artist's touch. It made me stop and really check out the book instead of just slipping it back in the box for return shipment. That was still my intention, mind you, because I didn't have a nickel to my name, and there was no *way* I could afford to buy a book even if it *was* cool. But that cover art...that blank gaze of that little boy, the creepy absence of pupils...wove its spell and seduced me. I was intrigued enough to open the book at random and flip some pages, and my eyes landed on this paragraph:

> The woman in the tub had been dead for a long time. She was bloated and purple, her gas-filled belly rising out of the cold, ice-rimmed water like some fleshy island. Her eyes were fixed on Danny's, glassy and huge, like marbles. She was grinning, her purple lips pulled back in a grimace. Her breasts lolled. Her pubic hair floated. Her hands were frozen on the knurled porcelain sides of the tub like crab claws.

Holy crap, *that* got my attention! I read the next paragraph detailing the little boy's horrified reaction to the corpse he's discovered, then the author nailed me with the kicker to the scene, a simple line that read, *"The woman was sitting up."*

That was my first introduction to Stephen King. Needless to say, the book never went back in the box. I read *The Shining* from cover to cover in a white heat, virtually in one sitting. As soon as I finished it, I turned back to the first page and *read it again*. After that I shared the book around with my high school friends until it was read to tatters and fell apart. (Of course I somehow found the money to pay for the

Introduction to *Knowing Darkness: Artists Inspired by Stephen King*

book after all—I probably scrounged it from my mom, I honestly don't remember that part of it. But I do know that a few years ago I bought another first edition of *The Shining* for my bookshelves—an exact duplicate of the one I'd received from the book club—and you can believe the replacement copy cost me a hell of a lot more than the first one did back in '77.)

Fate sometimes hinges on very small things. For me, the thing that opened the door to being a Constant Reader of Stephen King's words—and subsequently a colleague, and from there a devoted friend—is that an artist named Dave Christensen, sitting at his easel one day, made a creative choice not to paint eyeballs on a kid that appeared on the cover of a book that was shipped to me by mistake.

I send out thanks to the universe for happy accidents. And I send out thanks to that artist, Dave Christensen, wherever he is. Dave, you did a fine job. Though one *can't* judge a book by its cover, you honorably did what they hired you to do: you got me to at least *open* the cover and give the book a chance.

The Shining was another huge success for Steve—it's the novel that sent his reputation into the stratosphere and propelled him to brand-name author status. The man has been writing like Sisyphus rolling that fabled rock up that hill in Hades ever since...

...and that's a good segue for me to tell you why I think this magnificent, hernia-inducing book you're holding in your hands is such an impressive achievement. I'm certain that in the years since *Carrie*, with his publishing schedule seldom slowing for a moment, *Steve has single-handedly generated more damn artwork than any other writer since the dawn of time.* That's not hype. I doubt there's even a close second.

FRANK DARABONT

Think about it: every book he's ever written—a shitload of them, by my scientific count—has appeared in an endless variety of printings through the years, from humble paperbacks to the most grand and sublime limited editions. I'm stating the obvious, of course, but what you might not have considered is this: *all those editions of all those books have different cover art.* Further, consider that many of Steve's books contain lavishly illustrated *interior* art as well—which, to my knowledge, makes him almost unique among modern authors (and makes me certain he spent a lot of hours as a kid with a flashlight under his blankets poring over those stunning N.C. Wyeth illustrations in Robert Louis Stevenson's 1911 edition of *Treasure Island*). Then let's factor in all the art from all the *movies* spawned by King's work (again, a shitload)...*and* the fact that he's recently become a major force in the world of comic books with ongoing adaptations of his Dark Tower series and *The Stand*...well, the mind boggles, doesn't it?

For decades, Steve has created his very own industry when it comes to keeping artists employed. I defy *anybody* to come up with a total, in numbers, of pieces of art birthed into this world by the words and imagination of midwife Stephen King.

Go on, try—it can't be done. But while we mull the challenge, let's pause to doff our chapeaus to Jerad Walters, the publisher of this book, for having the brass cojones to give it a try. He won't get there either, not entirely—corralling *every* piece of King-related art would be like strapping on our wax wings and flying to the sun—but from what I've seen of the layout of this gorgeous and unprecedented book, Jerad's staked his claim to primacy and taken a huge and worthy bite

Introduction to *Knowing Darkness:*
Artists Inspired by Stephen King

out of the subject. That he succeeded in bringing this book into the world at all delights me, but that he has done it so thoroughly and so well makes me bow down to the man. I assure you without my having to ask him that it was not an easy task.

I say that based on my own fleeting experience. Let me share an anecdote with you that Jerad himself doesn't even know (but I guess he will after reading this): a few years ago, I phoned Steve King with what I thought was an inspired idea. The conversation went something like this:

> ME: "Steve! I have an idea for a book. Hang onto your hat, this one's a winner."
> STEVE: "Lay it on me."
> ME: "You know how much I love art, I know how much *you* love art. And I've been mulling how much amazing art has been generated by your work through the years, so many talented artists doing all this great work..."
> STEVE (slightly nervous): "Yeah?"
> ME: "I'm saying you should put all that art together and publish it as a huge book, call it *The Art of Stephen King*."
> STEVE (after a slight pause): "Jesus...you know how much *art* that is? Or the effort that would go into a book like that? *No way, Jose!* There aren't enough hours in the day, or days in the year! It would take forever! Sober up!"

Or words to that effect. (I'm paraphrasing from memory here, but I promise you the essence of the conversation is dead accurate.) And I had to concede that Steve had a good point: it would be an insane and *monumental* task. Who on earth could ever pull it off? Who on earth would ever be ambitious or crazy enough to even *try*? As I hung up the phone with Steve that day, he'd convinced me that that was the end of it, that no art book of the kind I was daydreaming about would ever exist. Case closed.

But here's what neither Steve nor I (slackers, we) had counted on: that a devoted publisher of high-quality limited-edition books named Jerad Walters would come along with the same idea (independently of me—let's be clear, I claim *no* credit for this) and not only *talk* about the possibility, but actually *do* something about it. Where I had dismissed my notion as wishful thinking, Jerad embraced his as inspiration. Where I had merely flirted with the idea, Jerad proposed marriage. Where Steve and I had clucked like chickens, Jerad saw an opportunity, hunkered down, and did it.

I want to thank you, Jerad, for being not just a talker, but a doer—for not just *having* the idea, but for *making it happen*. We owe you a debt, we lovers of both art and Stephen King the world over. The book I daydreamed about years ago, and was convinced I would never see, is now a reality thanks to you. The effort must have been staggering, but so is the result. You're a better man than I, Gunga Din. I salute you.

While I'm holding that salute, let me acknowledge the artists on display in this book. I can't help playing favorites and mentioning that two of them, Bernie Wrightson and Drew Struzan, are among my closest friends in the world. Like Steve King, they are the most good and loyal friends one could ask for—paragons of decency, kindness, reason,

Introduction to *Knowing Darkness: Artists Inspired by Stephen King*

enlightenment, and loving generosity. Drew and Bernie are brothers to me. They are also very high on my list of favorite artists of all time, and I'm never less than flabbergasted by the alchemy they create. I've been privileged to watch both of these legendary artists at work, and if you don't think *that's* cool, you don't know what cool is. For me, it's like watching angels dance.

All the artists in these pages deserve credit for what they've given us. They're the ones I spoke of earlier whose work has always tugged at my heart the most, the illustrators who've spent their lives rolling up their sleeves and meeting their deadlines, all too often laboring in obscurity but always caring deeply about their craft. They've drawn water from the well of Stephen King's imagination, drunk deeply of it, and created a sprawling body of artwork that enriches and delights the rest of us beyond any measure of thanks. How wonderful that we can now celebrate those artists in the pages of this book.

Spock's Not the Only One Who Can Mind Meld: Stephen King and the Telepathy of Writing

STEPHEN SPIGNESI

—*In memory of Rick Hautala*

"Writing isn't about making money, getting famous, getting dates, getting laid, or making friends. In the end it's about enriching the lives of those who will read your work, and enriching your own life as well."
—Stephen King, *On Writing*

What is humanity's greatest invention?

The use of fire, development of the wheel, and creation of the internet are all central to civilization, but the most important invention is one you probably don't think of because it is so common: language.

Any way you look at it, our invention of, first, spoken languages, and then written alphabets, must count as the single greatest development in humanity's history. Ever.

Writing crosses space and time. It allows us to speak to denizens of the future; it allows our ancestors to speak to us. Books are time machines. And, in its purest form, what is writing? As Stephen King likes to say, it's telepathy. It's one mind connecting to another. Yes, Stephen King, at his finest, can mind meld with his readers.

For years, I described the experience of reading King as one of being "pulled" through the book. It was as though we didn't see the words and the story just flowed into our minds. This is an astonishing ability for a writer to have. And Stephen King has it in spades.

How does it work? In many varied and wondrous ways.

I have been reading, studying, championing, and writing about Stephen King's work for more than twenty-five years. As a writer and a teacher of Composition and Literature at the university level, I have long recognized the literary merit of King's work, and have done my best to encourage those with a "he's only a horror writer" perception of King to look deeper. In this essay, I'll try to explain the workings, the functional elements of King's writing, and hopefully provide an understanding of just how he achieves that oft-elusive telepathy between writer and reader.

Rhetoric is everything these days. I teach two First Year Writing courses at the University of New Haven and both of them focus on Rhetoric. Rhetoric means argument and, in writing, argument means to debate, to discuss, or to persuade.

All writing has four universal elements: text, purpose, audience, and tone. Every piece of writing can be analyzed and deconstructed by those four elements:

> **Text:** What the piece is physically and in terms of compositional genre:
> - *The Shining, Under the Dome,* and *The Great Gatsby* are *novels*.

Spock's Not the Only One Who Can Mind Meld: Stephen King and the Telepathy of Writing

- "Gramma," "The End of the Whole Mess," and "All That You Love Will Be Carried Away" are *short stories.*

- *Apt Pupil* and *The Mist* are *novellas.*

- "The Love Song of J. Alfred Prufrock" and "Paranoid: A Chant" are *poems.*

- "Hey Jude" and "Hey Soul Sister" are *songs.*

- "President Obama's Second Inaugural" and "I Have a Dream" are *speeches.*

- *Wit, A Doll's House,* and *Fences* are *plays.*

- *The Matrix* and *Pulp Fiction* are *screenplays/movies.*

- This piece you're reading and "Ever Et Raw Meat?" are *nonfiction essays.*

Just as classical composers wrote within a particular format—opera, quartet, sonata, symphony, etc.—so, too, do writers write within a particular "text." The text of a piece is part of the vocabulary of writing.

Purpose: What the piece purports to do:
- The purpose of short stories is to *tell a story.*

- The purpose of nonfiction essays is to *inform and persuade.*

- The purpose of speeches is to *inspire and inform.*

- The purpose of a poem is to *stimulate emotionally intelligent thinking*; to tap into deeper feelings for which the compressed language of poetry is often the perfect vehicle for such enlightenment.

All writing has a purpose. Jokes (and yes, jokes are a "text"—they're written, aren't they?) hope to make you laugh, and so forth.

Audience: The intended reader of a piece. Audience is a relatively simple concept to understand. An editor friend of mine who has worked at many of the major publishing houses for years told me that the biggest mistake an unpublished writer can make when discussing his or her proposal is to answer the question, "Who's your audience?" with the ludicrous response, "Everyone!"

What my editor friend wanted to hear was "psychological thriller fans"; "mystery lovers"; "people who collect cookbooks"; "lovers of military history"; "biography readers"; etc.

Stephen King's audience is, first and foremost, his fans. His audience also consists of people who love a good story, and people who like an element of the paranormal, and horror in their tales. King's fans also include readers who greatly enjoy intensely character-driven narratives.

Tone: This is the rhetorical element that individualizes writers. In my writing classes, I teach that writing is comprised of mechanics, content, and style. (And yes, I deduct points for all mechanics errors: spelling, punctuation, grammar, etc. As George Carlin says in his epic poem, "I'm a Modern Man," "I'm new wave but I'm old school.")

Tone is where a writer's style manifests. Look at

Spock's Not the Only One Who Can Mind Meld: Stephen King and the Telepathy of Writing

this excerpt from King's nonfiction autobiographical writing tutorial *On Writing:*

> Mostly when I think of pacing, I go back to Elmore Leonard, who explained it so perfectly by saying he just left out the boring parts. This suggests cutting to speed the pace, and that's what most of us end up having to do (kill your darlings, kill your darlings, even when it breaks your egocentric little scribbler's heart, kill your darlings)... I got a scribbled comment that changed the way I rewrote my fiction once and forever. Jotted below the machine-generated signature of the editor was this mot: "Not bad, but PUFFY. You need to revise for length. Formula: 2nd Draft = 1st Draft—10%. Good luck."

Isn't your immediate response something along the lines of, "Tell me more"? He sucked you in immediately, right? In 108 words.

Here's another, also from *On Writing:*

> Talent renders the whole idea of rehearsal meaningless; when you find something at which you are talented, you do it (whatever it is) until your fingers bleed or your eyes are ready to fall out of your head. Even when no one is listening (or reading, or watching), every outing is a bravura performance, because you as the creator are happy. Perhaps even ecstatic.

Yes, goddamnit. Yes! He knows what I'm thinking! He knows how I feel!

Our enthusiastic response to King's friendly, smart, and informative advice is a response to his tone. I once heard an adage that I use all the time these days: "People like to work with people they like." Can we revise that to something along the lines of "People like to read people they like?" Notice I didn't say "*writers* they like." None of us (many of us anyway) actually personally know the writers we read. But we do recognize a friendly, compelling voice when we read one, and that speaks to the power of tone and style. Try to get through a Dave Barry essay (I particularly like "Driving While Stupid") or a Woody Allen essay (anything at all from *Getting Even, Without Feathers,* or *Side Effects*) without smiling or laughing. Tone is a fragile thing: Try too hard and it will elicit frowns rather than excitement, sympathy, or laughs. King is a master at using tone flawlessly.

Stephen King writes novels, short stories, poems, nonfiction essays, and screenplays. His voice is highly recognizable in whatever he writes. In fact, King's tone and style are so uniquely identifiable, he has become adjectival: Today, if I describe something to someone as "Stephen Kingesque," they know exactly what I mean. This does not happen with every writer. It happened with Dickens, with Steinbeck, with Eliot, with Dickinson, with Fitzgerald and, of course, with Shakespeare, but for many writers, their prose can be deceptively attributed to another writer and no one would know, or be able to tell, the difference. This is a function of tone.

It happens with movies, too. Directing and screenwriting are highly individual and quite identifiable. Scorsese

Spock's Not the Only One Who Can Mind Meld: Stephen King and the Telepathy of Writing

and Tarantino movies are unique to their creators. (Quentin Tarantino has also become an adjective: If you tell someone a movie is "very Tarantino," or "Tarantinoesque," they will likely know what you mean.)

What's special about Stephen King's style and tone is that his authorial voice changes depending on whether he's writing nonfiction or fiction.

His nonfiction voice is someone he has christened "Uncle Stevie." Uncle Stevie's writing is as close as any of us are going to get to sitting down with Stephen King and listening to him opine on all manner of topics. Uncle Stevie is friendly, conversational, wise, and a bit snide at times.

King's fiction voice, on the other hand, is, for lack of a better word, authoritative. And by that I mean, he rules the roost. He's in charge. He manifests the well-known analogy of the writer (artist, actually) being God (which came from James Joyce's *Portrait of an Artist As a Young Man*). King telling a story in the form of a novel or short story is so in charge he cannot be given anything but a reader's total attention.

As we writers have all been told since we learned how to hold a pencil, the beginning is everything. A killer first line will usually keep a reader with you...until you screw up.

Check out some of these randomly selected opening lines (in no particular order) from King novels, stories, and poems. Beneath each one is the inevitable question the line elicits from the reader:

- *Carrie*: "Nobody was really surprised when it happened, not really, not at the subconscious level where savage things grow."

What happened?

- **It**: "The terror, which would not end for another twenty-eight years—if it ever did end—began, so far as I know or can tell, with a boat made from a sheet of newspaper floating down a gutter swollen with rain."

What terror?

- **The Stand**: "Hapscomb's Texaco sat on Number 93, just north of Arnette, a pissant four-street burg about 110 miles from Houston."

What is going to happen at this gas station?

- **Cujo**: "Once upon a time, not so long ago, a monster came to the small town of Castle Rock, Maine."

What monster?

- **Misery**: "*umber whunnnn...yerrrnnn umber whunnnn...fayunnnn...*These sounds: even in the haze."

Why is he in a haze?

- **The Shining**: "Jack Torrance thought: *Officious little prick.*"

Uh oh. Why doesn't Jack like this guy?

- **Rose Madder**: "It was fourteen years of hell, all told, but she hardly knew it."

What kind of hell?

- **Bag of Bones**: "On a very hot day in August of 1994, my wife told me she was going down to

Spock's Not the Only One Who Can Mind Meld: Stephen King and the Telepathy of Writing

the Derry Rite Aid to pick up a refill on her sinus medicine prescription—this is stuff you can buy over the counter these days, I believe."

Uh oh. What's going to happen to his wife?

- **The Dark Tower: The Gunslinger:** "The man in black fled across the desert, and the gunslinger followed."

Why was he fleeing, and why was he following?

- **Gerald's Game:** "Jessie could hear the back door banging lightly, randomly, in the October breeze blowing around the house."

What's going on in this house?

- **The Mist:** "This is what happened."

What happened?

- **Under the Dome**: "From two thousand feet, where Claudette Sanders was taking a flying lesson, the town of Chester's Mill gleamed in the morning light like something freshly made and just set down."

What is going to happen in, or to Chester's Mill?

- **"Night Surf":** "After the guy was dead and the smell of his burning flesh was on the air, we all went back down to the beach."

How the hell did that happen?

- **"Trucks":** "The guy's name was Snodgrass and I could see him getting ready to do something crazy."

What is Snodgrass going to do?

- **"The Woman in the Room"**: "The question is: Can he do it?"

Can he do what?

- **"All That You Love Will Be Carried Away"**: "It was a Motel 6 on I-80 just west of Lincoln, Nebraska."

What happened at this Motel 6?

- **"Apt Pupil"**: "He looked like the total all-American kid as he pedalled his twenty-six-inch Schwinn with the ape-hanger handlebars up the residential suburban street, and that's just what he was: Todd Bowden, thirteen years old, five-feet-eight and a healthy one hundred and forty pounds, hair the colour of ripe corn, blue eyes, white even teeth, lightly tanned skin marred by not even the first shadow of adolescent acne."

Uh oh. What's this kid gonna get up to?

- **"Herman Wouk Is Still Alive"**: "Brenda should be happy."

Why isn't Brenda happy?

- **"Paranoid: A Chant"**: "I can't go out no more."

Why can't she go out no more?

- **"Dolan's Cadillac"**: "I waited and watched for seven years."

Waited and watched for what?

- **"The Man Who Loved Flowers"**: "On an early evening in May of 1963, a young man with his

Spock's Not the Only One Who Can Mind Meld: Stephen King and the Telepathy of Writing

hand in his pocket walked briskly up New York's Third Avenue."

Uh oh. What is this guy up to?

- **"The Bone Church"**: "When traveling to the heart of darkness, terror is not an emotion—it's a destination."

Oh shit. What's in the heart of darkness?

- **"The Man in the Black Suit"**: "I am now a very old man and this is something that happened to me when I was very young—only nine years old."

What happened?

- **"Strawberry Spring"**: "*Springheel Jack.* I saw those two words in the paper this morning and my God, how they take me back."

Why do those words take him back?

What is common to all of these openings?

They instantly elicit a mental response consisting of a question demanding to know more.

Not every writer can do that. Stephen King can, and his storytelling mojo is astonishingly present in just about everything he writes.

I've tried for quite some time to figure out how King does it. How does he combine just the right words to create that sense of bypassing the reading process and, instead, being telepathically linked to the book and King, and *experiencing* a story rather than "reading" it?

Part of it is what rhetoricians call *ethos*: that sense of credibility an author has for his or her readers. We know what to expect when we begin to read something new by Stephen King; that is, we may not know what it's about, but we're fairly sure we'll enjoy it, right?

But it's also about word choice and accessibility, i.e., ease of use. Novels like Umberto Eco's *Foucalt's Pendulum*, Tolstoy's *War and Peace*, Melville's *Moby Dick*, Faulkner's *The Sound and the Fury*, and, of course, James Joyce's *Finnegan's Wake*, while hailed (rightly) as great works of literature (and they are; I'm not denying their bounties) are, in a word, challenging. Some say "difficult"; it boils down to inaccessibility. Take a gander at this, the opening passage from *Finnegan's Wake*:

> riverrun, past Eve and Adam's, from swerve of shore to bend of bay, brings us by a commodius vicus of recirculation back to Howth Castle and Environs.
>
> Sir Tristram, violer d'amores, fr'over the short sea, had passencore rearrived from North Armorica on this side the scraggy isthmus of Europe Minor to wielderfight his penisolate war: nor had topsawyer's rocks by the stream Oconee exaggerated themselse to Laurens County's gorgios while they went doublin their mumper all the time: nor avoice from afire bellowsed mishe mishe to tauftauf thuartpeatrick: not yet, though venissoon after, had a kidscad buttended a bland old isaac: not yet, though all's fair in vanessy, were sosie

Spock's Not the Only One Who Can Mind Meld: Stephen King and the Telepathy of Writing

sesthers wroth with twone nathandjoe. Rot a peck of pa's malt had Jhem or Shen brewed by arclight and rory end to the regginbrow was to be seen ringsome on the aquaface. The fall (bababadalgharaghtakamminarronnkonnbronntonnerronntuonnthunntrovarrhounawnskawntoohoohoordenenthurnuk!) of a once wallstrait oldparr is retaled early in bed and later on life down through all christian minstrelsy.

As a mental exercise...okay. As the opening to a compelling, enjoyable narrative, not so much. There is a place for studying literature in the great endeavor of human scholarship, but sometimes we just want a great story, right? And King, while possessing literary skills and enormous writing talent, can provide said story in an enjoyable accessible manner. To wit: this excerpt from that most teachable of novels (and I can attest to its academic viability, for I have taught it in my Stephen King course), *The Shining*:

>Jack Torrance thought: *Officious little prick.*
>Ullman stood five-five, and when he moved, it was with the prissy speed that seems to be the exclusive domain of all small plump men. The part in his hair was exact, and his dark suit was sober but comforting. I am a man you can bring your problems to, that suit said to the paying customer. To the hired help it spoke more curtly: This had better be

good, you. There was a red carnation in the lapel, perhaps so that no one on the street would mistake Stuart Ullman for the local undertaker.

As he listened to Ullman speak, Jack admitted to himself that he probably could not have liked any man on that side of the desk—under the circumstances.

Ullman had asked a question he hadn't caught. That was bad; Ullman was the type of man who would file such lapses away in a mental Rolodex for later consideration.

"I'm sorry?"

"I asked if your wife fully understood what you would be taking on here. And there's your son, of course." He glanced down at the application in front of him. "Daniel. Your wife isn't a bit intimidated by the idea?"

"Wendy is an extraordinary woman."

"And your son is also extraordinary?"

Jack smiled, a big wide PR smile. "We like to think so, I suppose. He's quite self-radiant for a five-year-old."

We're right there, aren't we? We're in the office with that officious little prick Ullman, and we're also inside Jack's head. We don't have to stop, intellectually puzzled (and with the appropriately bamboozled, at-a-complete-loss expression on our face), and wonder what "rory end to the regginbrow was to be seen ringsome on the aquaface" means.

Spock's Not the Only One Who Can Mind Meld: Stephen King and the Telepathy of Writing

All this deconstruction and analysis aside, though, I think the most important thing to remember is that reading Stephen King is what reading for pleasure is all about. Sure, he may tackle deep moral questions and spur us to reflect on the nature of good and evil, but in the end, it's the story that matters. And this is something King himself has said repeatedly throughout his career.

King's incredible narrative charisma hides in plain sight. We have the words right in front of us and, yes, we can take paragraphs apart and study their inner workings and try to understand what makes them so magical. Books are, as King says, a portable magic, and sometimes we want to know how the magic works.

But ultimately, who cares? Who cares how he does it? Is knowing how the actual writing was done going to make the story better? If you're a writer, I suppose studying King is like being an architectural student just starting out and gazing up at cathedrals and trying to figure out how they were designed and built.

But do we really need to see behind the curtain? Isn't it enough to know that Oz is working and that the results of his efforts appear regularly?

As an English teacher whose job it is to understand how writing happens, I say yes, it is enough to know that Oz is working, and on my calendar are the release dates of his latest creations.

Again: *sometimes, that's enough.*

Disappearing Down That Rabbit Hole

JUSTIN BROOKS

Let's get it all out there in the open: collectors are a weird bunch. Not just book collectors or Stephen King collectors, but toy collectors, collectors of vintage 78 records, movie memorabilia collectors. Just try engaging in a conversation with someone who collects something passionately and start discussing their favorite subject. This individual is going to scoff at you for your lack of knowledge on the subject or bore you for hours on end with an endless stream of seemingly useless (but no doubt frighteningly accurate) information on pre-Civil War tax stamps. Trust me, I know. I am one of those folks.

I'm a collector of music, both digital (for those pesky download-only rarities) and physical (a dying breed, unless you like vinyl). But if you are reading this book, you might know me as a Stephen King collector. Now, my "collection" is very different from those of the super-collectors in that, at this point, if I have a photocopy of it, then I'm content as far as research purposes go. Besides, some of the stuff that I use for my research is only available in facsimile format (more on that later).

Due to the sheer amount of work that King has published (novels, short stories, poems, screenplays, recipes, and approaching 1,000 non-fiction pieces), his extremely dedicated fans (of which there are many) are put into a unique situation in deciding what exactly they want to collect. Not only is there a vast amount of material available (or sneakily unavailable), but there are many "states" of each book and limited editions of the novels and of anthologies containing his work. To my knowledge, no other author in the same arena of popularity as King has such a wide range of limited editions of their work. Of course, some of them want to have everything. Those fit into a Venn diagram where the intersecting circles consist of OCD, Stephen King Fan and Collector.

Note: For the purposes of this essay, I am going to exclude anything that does not contain actual writing by King: books about King, home media, promotional material, etc.

The first thing a collector needs to begin with is King's actual books: novels, non-fiction books, and collections. First and foremost, any real collector will be interested in obtaining first U.S. editions of all of these. While British (and sometimes non-English language) first editions are sometimes more collectible/valuable, the United States is King's home country and these should be the cornerstone of any good collection. Sometimes, the British edition is published first (if only by a day) and this can become what bibliophiles consider a World's First Edition. Some collectors who are strictly interested in TRUE first editions may want to adjust their collections thusly. Without getting into limited editions or proof copies at this point, you then have less desirable further printings: trade paperbacks, mass-market paperbacks, large print editions, movie tie-in editions, reprints by another publisher, "anniversary" editions with new content. At this point, you need to set your criteria. Do you want to own every edition or state of all proper King books or even of a particular book (perhaps your favorite)? Do you simply enjoy the different cover artwork? At this point, it is up to the collector where (or if) to draw the line. Most people are happy with a U.S. First Edition and maybe a U.K. First Edition. Obviously, any edition that contains new material (a new introduction, revisions, etc.) would be desirable as well, no matter the format.

Under the category of "books by King," we also have limited editions. At least half of King's books have had some sort of limited edition published either upon release or sometimes even years later. Invariably, these limited editions exist in different states (numbered, lettered, deluxe, etc.). Some collectors are going to be interested in owning each state. It gets somewhat more complicated if you consider that most of these limited editions also include "out-of-series" copies that aren't necessarily letter or numbered (but can be) and are used as replacements for damaged books or copies reserved for the author, publisher, artist, etc. Some of these can be very expensive and hard to obtain. One oft-cited example is the lettered (26 copies), asbestos-bound edition of *Firestarter*, which can fetch upwards of $15,000.00. Even if one is able to afford the exorbitant price, there are so few (and just enough collectors), that it might take the passing away/estate sale of a collector for one to even make its way onto the market.

Finally, we have proof copies. These books, for the most part, also fall under the "books by King" category that I have defined. Proof copies are highly collectible because the print run for these editions is usually very small (sometimes less than 100). Like first editions, there are usually proof copies for both the British and American editions. It is important to note that there are oftentimes various states of a proof. One interesting variation on the *Blaze* proof simply involved the price that was stated on the cover. The edition with the updated price was much more valuable than the earlier one. Also, in this category you have various bound or unbound states (folded and gathered sheets, blue lines/printer's proofs) of the book that are usually reserved for internal circulation within the publishing house. Naturally, these states are much more collectible/more valuable than the proofs (however scarce) that are distributed to media outlets. Sometimes, these manuscript copies are of earlier drafts of the book, but it is important to differentiate them from the original typescripts that we will discuss later.

King's short fiction is a very important aspect of his work. A great deal of it has been collected in various novella and/or short story collections over the course of his career, but some have not. And to further muddy the waters, there are sometimes two or more versions of a piece spread across various releases. When King publishes a brand new short story, it will more often than not appear in a magazine or anthology. Now, if you are King fan and/or collector, you are going to want to buy the first appearance for several reasons. First and foremost (and more on the fan side of things), you want to read the new King piece posthaste! Second (and more on the collector side of things), you will want this item in your collection unless you are content with the version that will probably appear in King's next official short fiction collection. I would imagine that in this case, the collector

Disappearing Down that Rabbit Hole

in question has consciously determined to not collect King magazines of any stripe. Finally, it is important to note that the version that will eventually appear in a King collection (excluding any uncollected work) may be different from the original appearance. These differences can be as simple as the altering of only a few words to a complete overhaul of the entire appearance, making it almost a different story entirely. To drive the most stout-hearted collector insane, you even have stories like "It Grows On You" that was published in two different versions before another revision was finally collected in *Nightmares & Dreamscapes.*

If all of the above sounds like we are going a bit overboard (and it might to the average person), then this will be the point that we start to disappear down the titular rabbit hole. There are a small handful of fiction pieces that, for whatever reason, King has decided not to collect and will remain a little bit hard to find. Now, some of these pieces may be reprinted in another anthology or magazine, but that is not always the case. Any true King fan will want to have all of these in their collection.

This is not necessarily the end of the line, because we also have excerpts and extracts from longer works (mostly novels) that some justification can actually be made for collecting. With the case of items like "The Bird and the Album" (an excerpt from *It*), "Memory" (an excerpt from *Duma Key*), and "The Tale of Gray Dick" (an excerpt from *The Dark Tower V: Wolves of the Calla),* we have pieces that are vastly different from their later appearance as parts of those novels. Any King fan worth their salt would want something like that, right?

Finally, there are some collectors who are interested in ANY reprint of a King piece. Some of King's more popular stories are reprinted dozens of times, everywhere from college textbooks to straight-to-remainder anthologies of absolutely little value. These can be seen as both the bottom of the barrel and the end of the line. While on the subject of King's short fiction, it is important to note that there are sometimes highly collectible limited editions of some of these anthologies, featuring the usual draws: signatures by King (and others), beautiful artwork, high quality construction, etc.

Collecting King's non-fiction work is most assuredly the next level of King fandom. It's a knotty, frustrating, but ultimately rewarding endeavor. At the time of writing, King's individual non-fiction pieces number almost 900. This is a complete sphere of King's writing that is often ignored or overlooked by the general public and sometimes, even King's hardcore fans. Noted King researcher Rocky Wood and I wrote a book for Cemetery Dance Publications called *Stephen King: The Non-Fiction* (published in 2008) that attempted to discuss every one of those pieces to date. Now, some of these are excerpts from his longer fiction works (still collectible, as mentioned earlier), introductions, afterwords, author's notes, etc. to his own work, so chances are you'll already have them, although some of them are only in certain editions of those books. See what I mean?

But let's talk about the non-fiction pieces that exist outside of King's official book canon. There are literally hundreds upon hundreds. These range from letters to the editor (of newspapers and magazines) predating even the publication of his first novel, *Carrie*, to several actual columns that King has written ("The Pop of King"; "King's Garbage Truck"). Some of these are incredibly easy for collectors to obtain copies of, such as copies of *Entertainment Weekly* (where King had

Disappearing Down that Rabbit Hole

his "Pop of King" column and many other pieces published), which were available by subscription, newsstand or for purchase on the Internet for a few dollars apiece. Original copies of others are almost impossible to track down. Originals are very important to the collector of course, so these can sometimes present an issue. Publications like *The Maine Campus* (college newspaper) and *The Drum* (high school newspaper) are very rare indeed. Oftentimes, with items like these, there is only one copy extant and that is owned by a King collector. Sometimes, that single copy is in the archive of a school, historical society, library, newspaper or individual. If this is the case, you are only likely to obtain a photocopy from a helpful person who works there (provided you know exactly what it is you are looking for). The same is true of some of the fiction pieces that fall into that category. If only a single copy is in existence, then anything other than a photocopy is impossible to obtain.

Even collecting in an area as specific as non-fiction written by Stephen King can get complicated, and I'd like to use several examples to illustrate this point. Stephen King wrote a letter to the editor of *TV Guide* magazine in July 1968 and they published it. How this piece even came to light is a mystery to me (I have written about it in my books however), but it is important for several reasons. First and foremost is the date of publication. For a long time, it was considered to be King's first officially published non-fiction piece (yes, letters to the editor count as non-fiction pieces in our world). This is excluding some "self-published" pieces that, while officially recorded in my bibliographic chronology, couldn't necessarily be considered official publication by a collector (as they cannot be officially obtained) and certainly cannot be considered as widely published, although the same argument could arguably be made about the pieces in *The Drum*. But, on the other hand, they certainly cannot be considered as unpublished, but merely very rare. This status was later proven to be false because earlier pieces were discovered in his college newspaper (*The Maine Campus*), a local Lisbon Falls weekly newspaper (*The Enterprise*) and a high school newspaper (*The Drum*). Do you see what I mean about things becoming complicated? Second is the content. Even someone only vaguely familiar with King's views on violence portrayed in the media (through interviews, essays, etc.) will recognize that this is a topic he keeps returning to again and again. The example here is one collector whom I know personally that wanted to collect every version of the July 13-19, 1968 edition of *TV Guide* magazine. He had discovered that, even in 1968, there were different regional versions of the magazine and thought that the first widespread publication of a King non-fiction piece was important enough to warrant collecting all that he could get his hands on. To date, these included sixteen separate regional variations, which I will list here to provide a sense of scope to this sort of thing: Western New York State; Eastern New York State; Southern Florida; Manitoba-Saskatchewan; Iowa; Central Indiana; Missouri; Western New England; Southeast Texas; New York Metropolitan; Washington State; Georgia; Carolina-Tennessee; Kansas City; Wisconsin and Northern Illinois. Despite several earlier pieces that were discovered, this can still be considered the first "major" appearance. Also, I am quite positive that there isn't any King collector far enough gone to want every regional edition of later *TV Guide* appearances. Even though the "Before the Play" excerpt and accompanying introductory note (three in one shot: short fiction, excerpt, and non-fiction!) are very interesting, I am sure there were many more regional variations of *TV Guide* in 1997 than there were in 1968, and the diminishing returns of such an endeavor simply would not be worth it. One interesting thing to note is that I paid $50.00 for a copy of one of those in the early 2000s, thinking that it would be worth at least that much due it being completely unknown (at the time) and what I perceived to be rarity. Ultimately, the Internet proved me wrong. At least fifteen other copies went up for sale in the years hence and none of them sold for $50.00. It certainly is interesting how many people saved 40+ year-old issues of *TV Guide* magazine and how many of those actually thought to sell them. Almost none of the sellers were even aware that there was a short letter by a then unknown (college age) Stephen King within.

I know all collectors want to have at least one original copy of each desired appearance in their personal collection, but sometimes that is simply not possible. I'd like to highlight a couple types of instances where that is the case. The first involves photocopies of items from newspapers and the second involves the actual original manuscripts of King's work.

In the course of my work on *Stephen King: A Primary Bibliography of the World's Most Popular Author*, I noted that King had written for a weekly newspaper called the *Lisbon Enterprise* based in the small town of Lisbon Falls, Maine. In his memoir/creative writing textbook *On Writing*, King himself talks about how working with John Gould at the newspaper was one of the formative experiences of his early writing career and arguably his first professional writing gig. Specifically, King talks about an article he wrote about a local Lisbon High School basketball game and even details a sidebar article to the piece about a basketball record set by a player named Robert Ransom. In September 2005, my fellow King colleague (and *Stephen King: The Non-Fiction* co-author) Rocky Wood was actually traveling and doing King research in Maine when I met with him and asked him if he could put it on his agenda. Rocky spent days traversing the back roads of Maine looking for a library that had back issues (either physical or microfilm) of the *Lisbon Enterprise*. None of those libraries had copies. Finally, he ended up at the Lisbon Historical Society, which had an incomplete back catalog of that newspaper. The remaining extant issues had not been archived on film or digitally and were literally falling apart. Ultimately, Rocky did not find the two pieces that we were looking for as that issue did not appear to exist in the archives. In fact, unless someone has old copies of the newspaper that haven't yet turned to dust, it is possible that they are lost forever. The *Lisbon Enterprise* no longer exists, John Gould passed away in 2003, and apparently, there are no existing archives outside of the partial run stored at the Historical Society. This story does have a happy ending, as Rocky was able to find two previously unknown pieces. One was "Progno For Tourney Go: Steve Thinks Chances Slim" from the February 24, 1964, issue of the newspaper. This is a short piece about the prospects for Lisbon High School's basketball team. The second piece was "Tit For Tat At Tourney: Lisbon High Hot And Cold," from the February 27, 1964, issue which recounts two Lisbon High School basketball games. These pieces are King's first known professional appearances and they were not self-published like *People, Places, and Things*, "The Star Invaders," etc. For a collector or a completest (they can be different), the only way to obtain this piece is a trip (or friendly phone call or e-mail) to the Lisbon Historical Society. Try to get copies before the originals totally disintegrate! A completest such as myself is happy, because all I need is a photocopy to add to my archives. A collector would likely be at least a little bit frustrated because they can never own an original copy of the newspaper where this piece first appeared.

Finally, you have actual manuscripts. Over the years, typewritten manuscripts (usually with King's handwritten corrections and/or notes) have appeared for sale in various venues. Often, these come to light in auction booklets and are sold that way. Over the years, certain high profile limited edition booksellers have dealt in original King manuscripts as well. In these instances, they are dealing exclusively with private collectors who are interested in and can afford such high-priced items. While I know a few of these so-called "super-collectors," there are also a few whose names are completely unknown to the close-knit King community and since they prefer to deal in private, some of their acquisitions (at least as far as the realm of original manuscripts) only come to light years later, if ever. Sure, there are drafts of the published novels out there in collectors' hands and while those would be extremely interesting to any obsessed King fan, the real gold is in completely unpublished (either complete or incomplete) material.

One of the best examples is King's incomplete story "Keyholes," written in 1984. It consists of two and one-half handwritten pages contained in a notebook that was donated to the American Repertory Theater Benefit Auction (May 1, 1988). This notebook also contains several notes from

King to himself and to his wife, Tabitha; King's handwritten outline revision (unused) of the *Silver Bullet* screenplay and twenty pages of King solving algebraic equations by hand. A prominent King collector now owns this notebook and I understand it has changed hands several times since the original auction.

Two other examples deal with typewritten manuscripts for unfinished novels. The first is an incomplete novel that King was writing for his son Owen in 1983 titled *The Leprechaun*. King had written several pages of the story in longhand in a notebook and then transcribed them. While on a trip to California, he wrote about 30 more pages of the story in the same notebook, which was lost off the back of his motorcycle (somewhere in coastal New Hampshire) on a trip from Boston to Bangor. The only part that still exists today is the 5 typescript pages that had been transcribed. The 5 pages, plus a 3-page cover letter to a senior editor at Viking are now owned by a King collector. The second is *Wimsey*, from 1977. This is King's attempt at writing a mystery novel based on Dorothy Sayer's character of Detective Lord Peter Wimsey. The 15 typescript pages (a fourteen-page first chapter and the first page of the second chapter), plus a 2-page cover letter to William G. Thompson (King's editor at Doubleday at the time) are now owned by a King collector.

While photocopies of the extant portions of *Wimsey* and *The Leprechaun* do circulate among King collectors and hardcore fans so that the more determined and interested individual might be able to obtain a copy, there are surely other pieces that are completely unknown to pretty much everyone in the King community. I believe the best and most recent example is the case of "After the Play." It has long been

Disappearing Down that Rabbit Hole

known that the prologue ("Before the Play") and epilogue ("After the Play") of King's classic novel *The Shining* were shaved from the finished product to shave one dollar off the cover price (something that would never happen now). While the prologue was eventually published in *Whispers* magazine in 1982 and in abridged form in *TV Guide* in 1997, every King resource (including my own Bibliography) listed the epilogue as "lost." It has recently come to light that "After the Play" is apparently not lost at all. Although, it is unlikely that King's office even has a copy in their files (which is not that uncommon in these cases, although Rocky and I try to supply them with copies of the rare pieces that we uncover), it appears likely that it is in the hands of one of the private collectors mentioned earlier.

A source of mine forwarded me a scan of an auction listing from September 1993 (Pacific Book Auction Galleries) for "The Collection Formed by John McLaughlin of the Book Sail." The description in the auction booklet is as follows:

King, Stephen. *Before the Play*. 44 page typescript, plus the unpublished *After* (epilogue), a 4 page excerpt apparently from the manuscript of *The Shining* (numbered 517-520), all hand-corrected by King. Accompanied by a 2 page T.L.s./ formal agreement from King's then-agent Kirby McCauley to Stuart David Schiff, signed by King, McCauley & Schiff. The previously unpublished "prologue" to *The Shining* was cut from the published book by agreement between Doubleday & King, evidently because it would have added sufficient page count to add $1.00 to the retail cost of the book. This "prologue" was published by Stuart Schiff in the "Special Stephen King" issue of *Whispers* in 1982. The "After" segment is also signed by King, dated 10-13-84. Near fine.

I have spoken with the collectors that I am in contact with and Mr. Schiff, but nobody claims to have this piece or knows what became of it. Hopefully, this piece will one day surface again in a sale or in the hands of a collector who is at least willing to share a photocopy for archival purposes.

At some point, you are going to disappear down the rabbit hole, so there is no need to fight it. As with all of my hobbies, this happened to me. At some point, I decided that since most of the non-fiction pieces I was obtaining were for research purposes only, photocopies were good enough. The fact that a lot of the items that I have are only available in facsimile form due to their rarity also helped. Also, I sold almost all of my proof copies because I determined that a first edition was enough for me. To me, a trade paperback copy of the book that I had to treat with kid gloves but was essentially no different from a first edition (save a blander cover) was not something that I needed to use up my limited space and time. It did hurt me a little bit to sell them, but that only stands to reason for any collector of anything. Ultimately, my reader and collector sides will have to decide where (or depending on funds, if) to draw that line. You'll be deep in one of those underground tunnels by then anyway. Don't worry though. It's still fun.

The Politics of Being Stephen King

TONY MAGISTRALE

People read Stephen King for many different reasons. I suppose this is probably true for many important novelists, but I'm not sure how many authors get the range of readership that has over the years both blessed and cursed Stephen King's reputation. Each time I teach a course on King's fiction at the university where I work, I ask my students to tell me something about what kind of fiction they like to read. On more than one occasion, I have heard the response that King is the *only* fiction writer these particular students read. I'm not sure how many other writers can claim such an exclusive fan base, or how many of them would even wish to.

Over the years, Yale University professor and literary critic Harold Bloom has maintained what might generously be termed an ambivalent attitude toward the work of Stephen King. To date, Bloom has published with Chelsea House Publishers three editions of collected essays about King's fiction for which he has both edited and written Introductions; this suggests at least that he appreciates King's undeniable marketability, if not his significance as a member of the American literati. All three of Bloom's Introductions eerily resemble one another: while they acknowledge King as a popular novelist, in possession of narrative skills that appeal to an unsophisticated mass audience, they also ultimately conclude that his achievement is "sub-literary." Bloom intuits that King's work "has a certain coherence and drive," even going so far as to concede that while Carrie White "will not survive as a figure of American literature, she seems to have entered our folklore." At his most magnanimous, Bloom admits that King "has a kind of archetypal power of the image," a cryptic phrase by which I believe he means that King produces characters and situations that resonate powerfully with readers on an emotive, primal level. Less admiring, however, is Bloom's inability to "locate any aesthetic dignity in King's writing: his public could not sustain it, nor could he," and his caustic pronouncement that "King will be remembered as a sociological phenomenon, an image of the death of the Literate Reader."

Bloom's most disparaging observations, regrettably, have echoed through the musty halls of high school and college English departments in America and abroad, and they are most often reiterated by teachers who have never read a King book. Not only are King's fiction and film adaptations seldom taught in academe (with the notable exception of *On Writing*, the author's fine memoir about the craft of writing, which sometimes finds its way into a composition classroom), over the past three decades I have received complaints from students in high school, college, and even graduate school lamenting that their teachers and programs will not permit them to write about King's work for academic credit. The combination of being pigeon-holed in the academically disreputable horror genre, his popularity, his wealth, and his

The Politics of Being Stephen King

celebrity status have set up a hostile polarity between critics, like Bloom, who will never be able to reconcile popular writing with literature and the well-established cottage industry of literary, film, and cultural studies scholars who believe that Stephen King is a serious artist worthy of their consideration. The latter has found recent affirmation in the pages of *The New Yorker, Esquire,* and *The Atlantic* magazines, where King's essays and short fiction have appeared with increasing frequency since the mid-1990s.

Although Prof. Bloom would certainly disagree, it seems obvious that King's achievement is somehow different from and vastly more important than the canons of other enormously popular writers—such as Danielle Steele, John Grisham, and Nora Roberts—with whom King often shares a spot on the best-seller lists. Unlike the work of these other novelists, whose narratives strike me as highly repetitive and formulatic (a legal battle will always be central to resolving a Grisham novel, while Steele and Roberts appear firmly wedded to most of the predictable conventions of the romance genre), King is less easily pigeon-holed as a creative artist. While his fame admittedly rests on his gothic credentials, there are few contemporary authors writing better prison fiction—or, for that matter, Westerns. Moreover, very few novelists, even best-selling novelists, have managed to attain King's degree of success when their work was adapted into film. Only J. K. Rowling's Harry Potter series and J. R. R. Tolkein seem to have duplicated the same level of crossover interest. Steele, Grisham, and Roberts simply have had precious little of even their best fiction translated into enduring films. King, on the other hand, has had several novels adapted into movies that have already entered into the cinematic pantheon—which, incidentally, is not the case with any of the Harry Potter films—bridging the popular with the critically-acclaimed.

Stephen King represents one of the great American success stories, an embodiment of the Horatio Alger myth, rising from obscure poverty to *Forbes'* list of wealthiest American celebrities. At one point I remember reading that world-wide sales of King's books were second only to the Bible, and we know the latter had at least four co-writers. The demographics associated with Stephen King's success may indeed signal Bloom's death of the Literate Reader, but its converse may also be true. In the birth of the Non-Literate Reader, King's books are compelling enough that they have attracted people, like those students I mentioned earlier who sometimes find their way into my King class, and who normally do not read much of anything, let alone five hundred-page novels.

As for Bloom's abstract generalization that King's writing lacks "aesthetic dignity," one must give the Ivy League devil his due; there are few works he has published that would not benefit from the steely hand of a rigorous editor, as King tends often to overwrite, to add parenthetical remarks and an overdose of visceral violence that distract the reader from the narrative, and to conclude many of his longest books without the same level of intensity and dignity of focus with which he began them—I would recommend *The Dark Tower* as the most egregious example of this last point. Harlan Ellison seems accurate when he argues, "I can't think of any King novels with the possible exception of maybe *It* or the [first two] *Dark Tower* books, that could not have been told just as well as a novella." Moreover, his diction and sentence structures are seldom poetic—King is not a great prose

The Politics of Being Stephen King

stylist—primarily because he is a straight-forward storyteller where plot takes precidence over aesthetics, and where language serves primarily as a vehicle to pilot narrative, rather than as an end in itself. As the writer himself acknowledged to me in an interview several years ago, "I have no quarrel with literary fiction, which usually concerns itself with extraordinary people in ordinary situations, but as both a reader and a writer, I'm much more interested by ordinary people in extraordinary situations. I want to provoke an emotional, even visceral, reaction in my readers."

While King has often complained that critics do not treat his work as having lasting merit, he compulsively revises new editions to include contemporary popular culture references, rather than believing his texts are sacrosanct and conform to the reference choices originally made. And although it is true that King tended to receive disparaging reviews in the mainstream press for much of his early work, the *New York Times*' reviews of *Bag of Bones, Lisey's Story, Duma Key, 11/22/63,* and *Full Dark, No Stars* all treated these books as serious literary works of fiction, overlooking the commercial devices the writer still employs, even though these narratives would all be much stronger without them. King's reputation in both New York and Hollywood has seemingly reached the point where reviewers at least finally understand the relevance of Stephen King, that he has by now made an undeniable contribution to and impression upon American culture, and they politely ignore the clunky italics, parenthetical and sub-plot digressions, flabby paragraph structures, and made-up words.

On the other hand, when Mr. King is fully invested in a narrative, that is, when he is engaged in his role as a pure storyteller—the fabulously sinister history of the Overlook Hotel revealed in the scrapbook chapter (18) in *The Shining* or the use of a solar eclipse as a nuanced metaphor that deftly unifies the patriarchal abuses as well as the acts of female sexual violation and the dramatic emergence from its shadowy underworld common to both *Dolores Claiborne* and *Gerald's Game* spring to mind immediately—I can think of no more talented writer on the planet. King's ability to place the reader in the consciousness of a character, or to create and visualize a particular time and place, and then to invest that moment with significance that resonates throughout the remainder of the narrative, may be as close to "aesthetic dignity" as any prose writer is ever likely to get. These are examples of writing that I suspect any novelist serious about his or her craft would be proud to have depicted.

Furthermore, ask a King fan, or a film aficionado with an understanding of the horror genre or Stanley Kubrick's cinematic canon, and it's likely that he or she will tell you there is something special about *The Shining*. This novel may well be the representative Stephen King book that will endure as the writer's legacy one hundred years from now; it is certainly the King work most often taught in universities and high schools. And thirty-six years after the book became King's first hardcover bestseller, American culture still cannot escape its fascination with both the novel and Kubrick's film. More scholarship has been published about *The Shining* than all the other books and films made from King's novels combined. Even as I write this, Rodney Ascher's *Room 237*, a film exploring the range of symbolism found in Kubrick's adaptation, is receiving enormous critical attention from the American media.

The Politics of Being Stephen King

Although he never specifies exactly what he means when he predicts that King will be "remembered as a sociological phenomenon," I suspect Bloom's point is to relegate King's place in American popular culture to an ephemeral commodity of our disposable epoch that carries no real significance beyond its moment in time—maintaining similar weight to a corporate advertisement, or a new reality television program—and certainly not worthy of being recognized as literature. This may be why Prof. Bloom was so incensed when King won the National Book Awards' annual Medal for Distinguished Contribution to American Letters in 2003. Or perhaps Bloom was merely exhibiting his New Criticism prejudice, stirred to acrimony by the fact that Stephen King often incorporates issues such as race, politics, and social commentary into his writing, and therefore violates the New Critic's preference for literature that privileges tradition and inaccessibility over events that define the historical present. In the end, the fact that Harold Bloom has edited three collections of essays about King's canon and that he continues to pursue a vociferous crusade against him, strongly suggests, ironically, the ultimate endurance of Stephen King.

Bloom's dismissal notwithstanding, there are other, more insightful ways of interpreting King as a "sociological phenomenon." His novels and stories are not merely products of our times, they also reflect deeply and critically on the social topography of late twentieth-and twenty-first century capitalism. My 1988 book, *Landscape of Fear: Stephen King's American Gothic*, was the first effort to examine King's work as a critique of American institutions and platitudes, including but not limited to organized religion, governmental agencies, schools, and the military. In fact, my book maintains that the supernatural phenomena which occur in his narratives are most frequently manifest as a direct consequence of real breakdowns in American political and social institutions. In an interview with *The Paris Review*, King himself affirmed the crux of my reading when he noted, "If you go back over the books from *Carrie* on up, what you see is an observation of ordinary middle-class American life… What that shows about our character and our interactions with others and the society we live in interests me a lot more than monsters and vampires and ghouls and ghosts." While this is an acknowledgement that would certainly shock a majority of King's fan base and most definitely those English teachers that have dismissed the writer's work for the past four decades, it would only serve to confirm Bloom's reasons for repudiating King.

Although it is fair to say that Stephen King's personal politics have been consistently left-wing since his college days at the University of Maine—e.g., the monies he has contributed to leftist politicians and causes (such as his recent $3 million challenge to rebuild the Bangor Public Library), the launching of his own radio talk show in 2011 to balance the proliferation of right-wing radio, and his scathing public criticism of Republican ideology, tax disparities, and candidates—the way of the hero in his fiction is never through political solutions or compromise. Nor is it working through the system to establish democratically progressive values. Indeed, his characters tend to lean much closer to political anarchy; they refuse to adhere either to a superficial value system to which others maintain allegiance—patriotism, religion, imposed definitions of masculinity, morality, etc.—or to an abstract idealism that advocates applying the freedoms inherent in American democracy in order to enact social change. Instead, his central protagonists embrace an iconoclastic and individualized life code that the hero constructs and imposes for him or herself. So, while King may embody a leftist critique of mainstream American institutions and morality in his public statements and throughout his canon, he is at the same time staunchly conservative in his insistence that individuals must strive for independent self-actualization. It is remarkable to me that Clint Eastwood has yet to direct a King film or star in one; the two would appear to share a similar perspective in defining American heroism. David Punter sums up this contradiction eloquently when he states, "At the heart of King's fiction...is a truly liberal message which is in constant tension with the conservative lives he depicts, and it is this tension, which is ultimately political, that gives his work its resilience, its sense of a wider meaning and, in the end, a curious but undeniable grandeur."

Perhaps reflective of this conservative strain, King's heroes are typically simple men and women of few words, even when the hero, as often happens, is a professional writer. In contrast to the intrusive noisiness of evil, whether manifested in the abusive physicality of a George Stark (*The Dark Half*) or Jim Dooley (*Lisey's Story*), the insane chatter and brooding ruminations of Blaine the Mono and Mordred in *The Dark Tower*, or the obnoxious (albeit wickedly amusing) stream of sarcasm from Pennywise and Randall Flagg, the King hero lets his actions speak in place of words. *The Dark Tower's* Roland Deschain is certainly the archetype for these figures with his quiet interior focus and unwavering dedication to the Tower's Beams. Roland is not much of a negotiator; he is more comfortable in active opposition to authority—providing orders to his allies about how to conduct themselves in combat or planning an effectively gruesome battle strategy. As King informs us early in the journey, the gunslinger "had never been a man who understood himself deeply or cared to; the concept of self-consciousness (let alone self-analysis) was alien to him. His way was to act—to quickly consult his own interior, utterly mysterious workings, and then act." It should be argued that Roland is King's core avatar, a distillation of all the male heroes that populate the King canon. In the end, Roland emerges as another figure in King's gallery of American males, joining flawed but nevertheless heroic characters such as Mike Anderson in *Storm of the Century*, Stu Redman in *The Stand*, Johnny Smith in *The Dead Zone*, Ted Brautigan in *Hearts in Atlantis*, Paul Sheldon in *Misery*, Andy Dufresne in "Rita Hayworth and Shawshank Redemption," and Jake Epping in *11/22/63*. Not surprisingly, the typical heroine in King's universe is likewise a highly *masculinized* figure—similar to Carol Clover's construction of the "Final Girl" found in *Men, Women, and Chainsaws*, the sole survivor in the slasher genre—insofar as she maintains a similar level of independence and willingness to resort to violent action to affect her own self-rescue. However, her motivations are always less inclined toward the macrocosmic epic quests of a Roland or Jake Epping, centering instead on defending herself and her children against the more immediate threats of impaired husbands and fathers. (King would thus appear to share yet another conservative value in his extreme dedication to the sanctity of American motherhood, since the preservation of the mother-child bond remains overwhelmingly the major motivation for actions and choices made by his heroine-protagonists.)

Roland is certainly beset with the most difficult of all their challenges: saving the Tower that essentially holds up

The Politics of Being Stephen King

the universe. But to a very real extent, he confronts the same set of problems that force all of King's heroes to embark upon their respective survival quests: he must do so because there is no one else who will. And like the other heroes in King's canon, Roland operates from a distinctly self-constructed code. Roland adheres to the position that life is endurable only if a man's will is maintained, if he controls himself and his environment, and if he maintains a separate place for this control apart from the collective will of others. Although more prone to violence than most of King's other heroes, Roland justifies his level of destructiveness in terms of the most expedient means to a justifiable end. And to be fair, Roland resorts so easily to violence because his enemies are themselves warped criminals resistant even to blunt reasoning.

Another way in which Roland comes to resemble the other heroes found elsewhere in King's universe is the manner by which his journey gives shape to his personality. King has often cited the influence of Joseph Campbell's *The Hero with a Thousand Faces* as a reference for the epic journey as an instrument in the hero's moral education. Like Andy Dufrense, who learns to express himself emotionally in spite of the injustice of his nineteen-year sentence at Shawshank, or the Free Zone leaders in *The Stand* who are at first wholly unprepared to assume the mantle of leadership roles in the post-plague world, Roland learns valuable life-skills from his experience. Just as Father Callahan undergoes a metamorphosis during his years in exile, Roland's personality likewise modifies as a result of his relationship to others. His complicated love for Eddie and Susannah grows in depth and intensity as the story progresses; he is properly educated in virtues such as friendship and sacrifice, but also in the awareness that the quest to find the Tower is just as important as the Tower itself. Additionally, in the gunslinger's obvious paternal role with Jake, Roland demonstrates an evolving willingness to sacrifice himself for the child, such as in his compulsion to comb the booby-trapped city of Lud in order to rescue Jake from Gasher and Tick-Tock Man in Volume Three, *The Waste Lands*. Perhaps the single most compelling feature of the King hero-protagonist is finally the manner in which the reader witnesses a satisfying evolution from selfishness to teacher and nurturer. The King hero typically emerges as a highly flawed being, fiercely independent and prone to anti-social behavior. But in the course of the narrative, friendship and love smooth out his edges, revealing the potential human being beneath.

The impact of Stephen King's career on American culture is difficult to measure. We have some crude benchmarks, such as the incredible number of book copies sold or the fact that many of his nearly one hundred film adaptations have included some of the most accomplished actors, directors, and screenwriters working in Hollywood. Philip Simpson alerts us to the fact that "King's cultural influence is apparent in the number of allusions to him and his work that appear in film, television, music, and novels." His unprecedented success, both financially and as a horror writer, is at least partly responsible for the opening every week of a new horror film at the local multiplex. Moreover, a generation of writers and filmmakers have now grown up reading and watching King novels and cinema: Eric Rickstad has told me that King's gothic themes and plotting techniques were an undeniable influence on his first novel, *Reap*; Justin Cronin's best-selling

The Politics of Being Stephen King

vampire novel *The Passage* is a homage to *The Stand*; while the majority of horror films made in the past thirty years that feature a haunted house or remain vigilant to a postmodern film-music aesthetic in which the score stands as an image in its own right are, to greater or lesser degrees, indebted to Stanley Kubrick's adaptation of *The Shining*. Although he has emerged as a product of the fertile American gothic imagination that takes us back to Poe and Hawthorne, King has ultimately transcended the genre and become a spokesman for his times. Similar to the impact the Beatles created and still manage to exert, or Steve Jobs's visionary proliferation of Apple computer technology, Stephen King is that rare occurence whose art has reflected—at the same time that it inimitably shaped—the larger culture of which he is a part. If this is what happens when a novelist becomes a "sociological phenomenon," then future readers can only hope for more sociologists like Mr. King.

The Adventure of Reading Stephen King

MICHAEL R. COLLINGS

Reading Stephen King has been an adventure that has lasted over thirty years. It has given my life a degree of direction, both personally and professionally; it has helped me hone my own writing skills to no small measure; and it has provided countless hours of sheer pleasure.

I came to Stephen King's novels almost accidentally while teaching "Myth, Fantasy, and Science Fiction" during one of my first summer sessions at Pepperdine University. After class one day, one of the sharper students—whose judgment I had grown to trust over the weeks—approached me and asked if I had read anything by Stephen King.

I hadn't.

"Well," he said, with a confidence that belied our student-teacher relationship, "You should." In addition, he added that I should begin with one text in particular: *The Dead Zone.*

At that point, I was aware that Stephen King was a writer, that his works were generally categorized as "horror," and that he was selling quite well. I had even considered buying one of his books from the Science Fiction Book Club a few months earlier—but I had to admit that the cover illustration of two men (although the species of one remained indeterminate, due to the extended beak he/it seemed to have) hacking away at each other with swords while wearing odd clothing and ridiculously pointed shoes had turned me away. Other than that brief almost-encounter, I had not even thought about him.

But I trusted my student's advice.

That summer I read Stephen King—*everything* I could get my hands on by Stephen King. Fortunately, there weren't (yet) that many titles to locate; but after reading *The Dead Zone,* I began searching out the others.

When I finished with the King books, I looked further. I read Robert McCammon; I read Dean R. Koontz; I read James Herbert. I even read books by a few writers that I won't name (largely because I found what they wrote to be nearly unreadable), because by then I had discovered something remarkable.

King, McCammon, Koontz, and a handful of others not only told good stories, but they told them *well.* Strongly enough that I could incorporate their novels into my classes whenever possible. Back then, there were few SF/F offerings in university catalogues and none explicitly labeled "Horror." But these guys…they knew how to write in ways that made storytelling as much an art as a craft, and their works could provide excellent models for classroom instruction.

•••

Over the next few years, reading Stephen King—and other contemporary fantasists—took on new importance

The Adventure of Reading Stephen King

as I began submitting papers to professional conferences: the International Conference on the Fantastic in the Arts (ICFA), originally held at Florida Atlantic University in Boca Raton, FL; the Western States Conference on Christianity and Literature at Whittier College and, a few years later, at Pepperdine; the Conference of the Rocky Mountain Modern Language Association in Salt Lake City, UT; the J. Lloyd Eaton Conference on Science Fiction and Fantasy at the University of California, Riverside. The subjects varied, but with each presentation, I felt my way deeper and deeper into the complexities of speculative fiction.

Then, in a very real sense, I found my path.

In 1984, I submitted two papers to the Fifth ICFA. Both were accepted—the first on one of the most eminent British science fiction writers, Brian W. Aldiss, and the second on... Stephen King.

Oh, and I found out just before setting out for the conference that *both* authors were planning on attending.

Thus I found myself presenting "Brian Aldiss: Cartographer" with Aldiss sitting at the back of the room, occasionally nodding sagely (*good!*) and sometimes looking slightly puzzled (*definitely not so good*). A day later I was sitting in front of a room, along with two other presenters, and, just as we were about to begin, in walked Stephen King and Douglas Winter, one of the first people to write a book on King's works. My paper was an essay in typical academic understatement: "Science Fiction into Fantasy: Stephen King's *The Stand*." I suppose that back then I thought I could resolve the problem of defining genres—especially a problem as knotty as the relationship of science fiction, fantasy, and horror—with a single essay about a single novel.

I will admit that it was more unnerving to read the paper with Stephen King in the room than it had been with Brian Aldiss, and I also admit to glancing up to check his facial expressions more than once. He didn't particularly respond to the paper...which I later decided was a good thing.

On Saturday evening, King gave his Guest of Honor address. I learned a number of things from it. I learned that authors don't always have control over their stories (something confirmed later when I began writing my own novels); in answer to the question "Why did you let Tad Trenton die?" he revealed that he didn't know that the boy had died until he was writing the passage in which paramedics try to resuscitate Tad, and King realized that ten minutes of story-time had elapsed without the boy taking a breath. Tad was dead. King repeated several times that he had never intended that but that the story required it. A follow-up question asked if King was bothered by the fact that in the 1983 film version of *Cujo*, Tad lives. He smiled that slightly off-sided smile he has and said that he was glad they had. Another question dealt with similar re-workings of his novels when they appeared as movies: did the alterations annoy him? In answer, he gestured to an imaginary shelf of books behind him and said, "My books—my words—are still there. No one can change them."

(Ultimately, I worked with many of the novel-into-film versions of King's stories, and every time, whether I appreciated the film [*Stand By Me* was great] or didn't [don't get me started on *Children of the Corn*]; whether King had no hand in the film at all, as in *The Lawnmower Man* films; or whether he was fully involved with them, as in *Maximum Overdrive*, his perspective remained constant. He is a storyteller. He tells the stories as they must be told. When someone else chooses to retell them as film, he holds no responsibility for what might happen.)

Another point he made during his address impacted me more personally. He was asked about the experience of listening to critics present academic papers on his books. Immediately, my ears perked up since I had been one of those critics. In answer, he calmly and lucidly explained where each of them had erred in their interpretations. By the time he finished with the second paper, I was anxious (*i.e.* scared silly) to hear what he might say about the third...mine. He said nothing. I was relieved, not so much because he had apparently found little to fault in my ideas but because I had—also apparently—not made too big a fool of myself.

(Some years later, an interviewer asked King a similar question about academics and their comments. He included in his answer a reference to my work as frequently containing good things, so I guess the ICFA paper had established a kind of common ground.)

During that same weekend, I had another experience, one probably shared by few other conference goers. Coming down the stairs one evening, I met Dr. Roger C. Schlobin, the then-president of the International Association for the Fantastic in the Arts (IAFA) and spearhead behind the conference. He invited me to the hotel bar for a drink "with a couple of friends." Now, I don't drink—never have. At the ripe old age of almost forty, I'd never even been in a bar. Roger knew that I didn't drink, so I figured that if he was all right with me sipping on a Seven-Up, I was willing to join him.

And Douglas Winter.

And Stephen King.

The four of us sat around one of those ridiculously tall bar tables for nearly an hour *just talking*. Not about the conference. Not about King's status as one of the preeminent horror authors of our time. Not about techniques of writing or the state of the industry or any of the things I might have imagined.

Just about *things*.

And I discovered, perhaps for the first time, the human being behind the façade of horror. I don't remember many details about the conversation, just my then-and-now impression of King as a consummate storyteller, even when simply relating an anecdote over a table in a bar.

• • •

The next year, 1985, I had just sent off the final manuscript for a study of Brian Aldiss's novels and was relaxing in an armchair, congratulating myself on having nothing to do, when the telephone rang. It was Ted Dikty, the owner of Starmont House, who had published my first book of literary criticism, *Piers Anthony*, two years earlier and would publish *Brian Aldiss* in 1986. He had some fascinating news.

Stephen King had just acknowledged the "Richard Bachman" pseudonym.

Initially, I was interested primarily because I enjoyed reading King's novels, and suddenly there were five more to savor. Then Ted got down to business. Several years before, Starmont had published *Stephen King*, a short study of King's works by Douglas E. Winter. In 1984, that study was expanded and republished by NAL as *Stephen King: The Art of Darkness*—arguably the first book-length study of his writings.

The upshot for Starmont House was that it now lacked a monograph on King. Since Ted liked my work on Anthony

The Adventure of Reading Stephen King

and Aldiss, he asked me to write a similar book on King. My answer: an immediate "Yes."

We chatted for a few more minutes, then Ted hung up. I retreated to my armchair and began mentally preparing for the book.

The telephone rang again.

It was Ted again. This time he had a slightly different proposal. Would I be up to first writing a study of the five Bachman novels? I said "Yes." Then he explained that, in order to catch the crest of enthusiasm for the pseudonymous books, he needed the manuscript within a month.

A month!

We talked, and after he promised to help me locate the paperback editions of several novels, I agreed. In July, 1985, following a rush-to-print by Starmont, *Stephen King as Richard Bachman* appeared.

By that time, Ted had expanded his initial invitation. Rather than my writing a book on King's novels, something like the original Winter study, he suggested a series of books covering—as nearly as possible—every direction in King's writing. I agreed and, again with Starmont's stellar support, over the next eighteen months or so completed the entire series: *Stephen King as Richard Bachman*, which became a Starmont bestseller; *The Shorter Works of Stephen King* (August, 1985), co-written with my student-turned-collaborator, David A. Engebretson; *The Many Facets of Stephen King* (September, 1985), an assessment of King's novels to that date; *The Films of Stephen King* (July, 1986), subsequently translated and reprinted in Germany; *The Annotated Guide to Stephen King: A Primary and Secondary Bibliography of the Works of America's Premier Horror Writer* (October,

1986); and *The Stephen King Phenomenon* (March 1987), including an essay on the recently-published *It*, several essays on King's critical reception, and a week-by-week tally of King's appearances on the national bestsellers' lists...itself, I think, a collation of some rather extraordinary data.

Ted had envisioned a complete line of King-*iana*: casebooks on every novel, with original essays by a range of scholars and critics; books on King's non-fiction and poetry; and concordances to everything King had ever written. Unfortunately, Ted passed away shortly after the initial series was completed, so we did not begin any new works.

In a sense, I was relieved. In addition to my full-time teaching responsibilities at Pepperdine and my equally pressing responsibilities at home, I had written or edited nine critical studies in less than five years, which entailed reading literally thousands of pages of novels, short stories, articles, essay, reviews, and even poetry. It had been exhausting.

And I had loved every moment of it, particularly because it had brought me even closer to understanding and appreciating King's genius...and his generosity. Through him, I received a copy of *My Pretty Pony* at a time when none were to be had. While writing *The Many Facets of Stephen King*, I sent chapters to him as I finished them. He was directing *Maximum Overdrive* at the time, and during off moments, wrote long responses to the chapters, often including insights that found their way into subsequent chapters. One day, I opened my front door to find a large box—perhaps a foot in each dimension—on my porch. It carried the return address: Bangor, Maine. Inside was a copy of the *typescript* for *It*, still among my favorite novels, several months before even the ARCs appeared.

The Adventure of Reading Stephen King

We corresponded fairly frequently. I contributed to *Castle Rock: The Stephen King Newsletter,* reviewing novels, stories, and film adaptations. And throughout, I never lost sight of the fact that I was sharing ideas with one of the seminal minds of our time, a writer whose words were helping to define American culture, with all of its failures and foibles, during a period of unquestionable change.

The leisure I had anticipated upon completing the Starmont series never materialized, however. King kept writing. I kept writing: *In the Image of God: Theme, Characterization, and Landscape in the Fiction of Orson Scott Card* for Greenwood Press (1990); and more articles, reviews, and essays, many concentrating on King.

•••

The next stage in my King-career began in 1995. I was corresponding with a King enthusiast, George Beahm, who had already published several King-related books that included a number of my pieces. This time, he was revising his pivotal compilation, *The Stephen King Companion* (1989), and wondered if I would write 1000-word critical assessments of *every* King novel to date: *Carrie* through *Insomnia*. The resulting essays ended up comprising some 40,000 words, nearly 40% of the published book, and gave me the unexpected opportunity to consider each book, in chronological order, re-reading many, discovering resonances and possibilities that had earlier eluded me. Increasingly, King's skill as storyteller, his perception as cultural critic, his concern for the everyday details of American life as well as for its sometimes-disturbing directions became clearer for me.

And he kept writing.

•••

Following Ted Dikty's death, Robert Reginald at Borgo Press acquired Starmont's backlist, including my series. In 1996, Borgo produced *The Work of Stephen King: An Annotated Bibliography and Guide,* with nearly 500 pages and twenty-six sections. More than an extension of Starmont's *The Annotated Guide,* this was an entirely new look at the phenomenon of Stephen King—what he had written, how much he had written, and how much had been written *about* him.

By then, I was so attuned to things-King that the sheer amount of materials did not surprise me. Then one of my colleagues asked me—as often happens in academia—the status of my current research. When I answered that I was preparing a primary and secondary bibliography of nearly 3,000 entries, he went pale, stared for a moment, and seemed to struggle to find his voice.

"For a *living* author?" He was stunned. Such a mass of information was unheard-of, even for most safely dead authors.

About the same time, my then-teenage second son came home chuckling from high school one afternoon. Given his near-hatred for the entire experience, that chuckle in itself was odd enough to merit my noting it. But the reason for his laughter turned out to be even more intriguing than the fact of it, particularly since it related directly to my own interests over the past decade and a half.

His junior English class was preparing to face the great unmentionable, the horror of the year—the dreaded *Researched Term Paper.* His teacher had dutifully handed out a list of acceptable subjects, all American authors. The students were told to submit proposals for papers discussing at least three works by a single author or one work each by

The Adventure of Reading Stephen King

three authors, combining the students' perceptions with relevant outside sources (this was in the "bad old days," so online resources, including Google and Wikipedia, were suspect).

During the discussion, one student noted that his favorite author, Stephen King, was not listed.

No, the teacher answered solemnly, and severely, King was indeed *not* included.

Another student noted that several other contemporary popular writers were also missing and asked why.

In response, the teacher informed the class that such writers were of interest only to readers unable to handle the more sophisticated expression of the "classics."

"In other words," the second student shot back, defending himself and his friends who read King and others, "we read them because we're too stupid to understand the classics?"

"Uh, no." The teacher backpedalled. Still, she went on in generalities about the lack of sophistication in contemporary popular writers, noting in passing that most students hadn't even considered using King as a topic for the paper until a few years before, when a professor from Pepperdine began publishing a flurry of books about him.

At this point, my son sat up and began paying close attention.

Then, the teacher continued, the professor made things immeasurably worse by holding literary discussion groups at the local library, actually *talking* with groups of high-school students (for school credits!) about King and his works as if they had literary merit.

Now my son was *really* paying attention, wondering if he should raise his hand and say, "That was my father," or wait it out and see what else the teacher would say.

He decided to wait it out.

By the end of the teacher's comments, the class was told bluntly that in spite of such distinctly peculiar behavior (fortunately isolated) in a college professor, there really wasn't enough criticism on Stephen King or other writers like him to merit including them on the list of possibilities for the term paper.

Not enough criticism!

After stifling my own laughter, I sat down and wrote a calm, courteous, gracious (thanks to having taught Business Communication for a number of years) note to the teacher, pointing out several of her errors: (1) That Science Fiction, Fantasy, and Horror did in fact include authors capable of highly sophisticated discourse; (2) That many of those authors, including Poe, Tolkien, and Lewis, were already in most senses "classics"; (3) That King, besides being prolific, was among the authors most widely read by high school students and that therefore it might behoove her as a teacher to have some sense of what they were *actually* reading, rather than just what they were assigned to read; and, most relevantly, (4) That sitting on my shelf at Pepperdine was a 500-page typescript, a quarter or so of which was devoted purely to secondary works on Stephen King.

My son delivered the note the next day. I suspect he rather looked forward to it.

That afternoon, he returned home...with another note, this one inviting me to speak to *all* of the juniors at the high school in a series of three presentations in the school library, to be attended by all of the English teachers. The subject: Horror as Literature.

If nothing else, the enthusiasm those students brought to the discussion, their obvious love of King as author and storyteller, and the excitement with which the teachers responded to the lively discussions that followed was worth the work of so many years.

•••

Borgo continued its practice of re-printing the Starmont books. In 1996, I revised *The Stephen King Phenomenon* as *Scaring Us to Death: The Impact of Stephen King on Popular Culture*. Again, re-writing the text allowed me to work with old materials and discover new ones: the book contains an essay on *The Tommyknockers,* one of King's most harshly criticized novels; a previously unpublished essay on some of his earliest publications; and an update to the bestsellers' index through June, 1996, including King's several unprecedented (at this point, one wishes for further superlatives) runs of *four titles* on the lists simultaneously.

When the Borgo backlist was acquired by Wildside Press in about 2006, it included all of my Starmont books, plus the Borgo editions. Beginning in 2007 new printings of all of them have been available as print-on-demand volumes, making all of my early studies accessible again.

In May of 2000, another horror-oriented small press, Overlook Connection Press, published *Hauntings: The Official Peter Straub Bibliography,* followed in 2001 by *Storyteller: The Official Orson Scott Card Bibliography and Guide,* the second in a trio of annotated bibliographies Overlook had contracted with me. The third was to cover—guess who?—Stephen King. *Horror Plum'd: An International Stephen King Bibliography and Guide* represented a thorough revisiting of all of the data in all of my previous bibliographies. Initially, it was to include primary and secondary materials; a second, companion volume was planned for secondary works only.

At over 600 pages, it was (and is, to date, at least) my definitive statement on the body of Stephen King's writing. Again, compiling it gave me the opportunity to re-read and re-assess and to catch up on everything King had written and published during the late 20th century, ending in 1999.

Perhaps more germane to this article, *Horror Plum'd* included as its introduction a new version of an essay published several years before, "Light Behind the Shadow Trapped Within the Words." Essentially, the essay argued that, far from being merely a monetarily successful genre writer—less-generous critics have used words such as *hack*—Stephen King consistently allies himself in his stories with one of the most enduring trends in human culture: horror, the fear of the unknown and the unknowable. Since then the essay has been further expanded as "The Persistence of Darkness" and connects King's dark vision with writers as disparate, yet as fundamental to Western literature as the author of *Beowulf*, the great Renaissance dramatists Christopher Marlowe and William Shakespeare, and—for me, at least—the finest poet in the English language, John Milton. Indeed, the first part of the title, "*Horror Plum'd*," came from the description of Satan in *Paradise Lost*. My subsequent collection, *Toward Other Worlds* (Wildside, 2010) examined even more such connections, as evidenced by its subtitle, "Perspectives on John Milton, C.S. Lewis, Stephen King, Orson Scott Card, and Others."

Finally—and yes, there is an end, or at least a pause, to this litany of titles—2011 saw the publication of the newly expanded, completely revised text of my first Starmont book, now appearing through Overlook Connection Press as

The Adventure of Reading Stephen King

Stephen King is Richard Bachman, an attempt to put King's forty-year-long career into some kind of perspective. But even that version was destined to remain incomplete, since just after I submitted the manuscript, King published yet another "Bachman" novel, *Blaze.*

•••

And, at least as far as mid-May of 2013, this ends an odyssey that began over three decades ago. At each stage in my professional life—whether teaching at Pepperdine, where I was viewed as an anomaly, a maverick, and a bit of an odd-ball; or writing as scholar, critic, bibliographer, poet, essayist, or novelist—Stephen King has cast a mighty shadow over what I chose to do.

The key word here is *chose.*

No one pressured me to work with King's fictions; if anything, fellow academics often urged me to follow more traditional paths. But as I explained to King in a letter many long years ago, I chose to write about his works, to immerse myself in his words, because I am convinced of their worth, their value as literature and as insights into humanity, and their sheer capacity for entertainment. I think they are—for the most part (but that's another essay)—not only *good writing* but *extraordinarily powerful storytelling.*

I am proud to have been associated with them.

Reading the Lost Works of Stephen King

ROCKY WOOD

Many dedicated fans ["Constant Readers"] think they have read all Stephen King has published—they may even own each of his novels and fiction collections. But, of course, they would be wrong. King has been professionally publishing works since 1967 and writing as many works of fiction that have not been published as those that have! Like any writer he will start a project but abandon it later as the right combination of story, character, and inspiration fails to appear on paper. And there are other works that have been published in a variety of venues but never "collected" in one of his books.

During research for my various books on King's works I've had the pleasure of reading perhaps more works of fiction and non-fiction by Stephen King than probably any single individual outside his immediate family. I say that to introduce the subject of this essay—which is the value that may be found in seeking out these obscure works of fiction.

That value lies chiefly in three areas:

An understanding of how King developed as a writer;

An understanding of the similarities and dissimilarities in these obscure works to his better known canon; and

As always with King, the pure joy of reading a King story for the first or, for that matter, nineteenth time!

Firstly, how do you find these works? There are three major ways—hunting down the published but uncollected stories; visiting the University of Maine's Fogler Library (with King's permission slip in your hand); and "trading" with other King fanatics.

The easiest of these three is, of course, finding the uncollected tales that have been published, and that are purchasable from the usual retailers.

There are a number of unpublished tales at the University of Maine, held in the Special Collections Unit of the Fogler Library at the Orono campus (King's alma mater). This well-appointed and quiet sanctuary holds King's papers, most of which were donated two decades ago. Most of them are kept in "restricted boxes"—to access those you need written permission from King—which can be obtained through his office if you present a compelling case (generally that you can prove you are a researcher). The Restricted works are as follows:

> *Muffe*—two snippets from an incomplete fantasy story. You can read about one section in *Stephen King: Uncollected, Unpublished* (Third Edition ebook from Cemetery Dance, 2011; Fourth Edition paperback from Overlook Connection Press, 2014) and see actual handwritten parts of the other section in Bev Vincent's *The Stephen King Illustrated Companion* (2009).
>
> *The Aftermath*—a post-apocalyptic novel.

Reading the Lost Works of Stephen King

Sword in the Darkness—a tragedy set around an inner city race riot.

An untitled and incomplete piece set in Huffman—King's early attempt to write what became *The Dead Zone*.

George D X McArdle—an incomplete novel set in the early years after the Civil War.

Charlie—an incomplete science fiction tale; *Mobius*—another science fiction story.

But Only Darkness Loves Me—a fragment written with his son Joe when the latter was very young.

I Hate Mondays—an incomplete story written with his son Owen when that son was also quite young.

"Comb Dump," "Chip Coombs," "The Evaluation," and "Movie Show"—all story fragments, the latter has strong autobiographic overtones.

And five pieces of non-fiction.

Also restricted are the following screenplays: *Something Wicked This Way Comes* (adapting Bradbury's classic), *Night Shift* (adapting three stories along with a new wraparound tale), and an incomplete teleplay about a haunted radio station.

The following screenplays by King are in publicly-accessible boxes—*Pet Sematary*, *Golden Years* (an obscure TV series), *Sleepwalkers*, *Desperation* (all of which were produced), and unproduced scripts for *The Shining* (Kubrick rejected King's version), *The Dead Zone*, *Cujo*, a movie version of *The Stand*, *The Shotgunners* (later developed into *The Regulators* novel), and a fragment of *Dolan's Cadillac*.

Trading with other King fanatics is obviously the hardest of the three. You have to establish yourself as credible super fan. Join King discussion groups, such as King's official website message board, Facebook fan groups, etc., and build relationships over a lengthy period. Never offer to pay, or accept an offer to sell copies—this material is all King's copyright. Trading the odd copy is generally acceptable; the exchange of monies is not, under any circumstances.

Some examples should suffice to illustrate how a reader will benefit from accessing, reading and studying an obscure or unpublished work.

Phil and Sundance

In April 2013 a man tried to sell an 82 page manuscript for a "novella that SK wrote about 1987." He claimed he came to own the manuscript for *Phil and Sundance* because he "was the lucky recipient of a Make-A-Wish Foundation wish to meet Stephen King when I was thirteen years old." He also published a scan of the first page. When queried King responded, "It's legit, all right, but it's hazy—All I remember is that it was about little people..."[1]

After some "negotiations" the manuscript was purchased by one of King's publishers—Cemetery Dance. King then authorized a copy be released to me to review. Later, his personal assistant posted this at the official website's message board: "I'm glad to hear Cemetery Dance was the one to obtain it as we trust them to do the right thing. I've known about the manuscript for quite some time as we have a copy in our files although we don't have the complete manuscript—ours end at page 101 but it is mid-sentence although there are

---

1 Personal correspondence with Rocky Wood, 18 April 2013

other unnumbered pages that may continue it." So, there are clearly two versions in existence. However, it is very unlikely King will ever complete the work.

• • •

The protagonist is Phil Wentworth, who lives in the familiar town of Derry. He is ten, tall for his age and overweight. Immediately there is a hint of the young Stephen King (although King was not overweight—just big for his age) and we are placed in the mind of a young person (just as we remember being young), one of King's greater skills. Sample this classic King: "Although he was cautious about who had (*sic*) admitted it to (some people would laugh and say you were a pantywaist), he liked school, especially math and geography." He also liked Song and Dance Interpretation, although the square dance unit had proved he was a nerd—"a beefy sonofagun who had to alamand (*sic*) left and dosy-do right with a partner who was three inches shorter and sixty pounds lighter than you."

Phil Wentworth is alone at home one afternoon when he finds his sister's cat attacking what turns out to be Sundance, a "Teeny" "barely six inches high," a miniature humanoid from a species "nearing extinction" from the depredations of "Bigs," particularly birds.

Delving into Bill the cat's mind (as King did so effectively with Cujo) we find he is astonished to find he's stalking a *Teeny*. "Hard to believe but absolutely true. Of course he had heard the birds talking, saying there was a tribe of them somewhere about, but Bill put little stock in what birds said, even fairly intelligent ones like robins. Bogie, his grandfather, had told him a great deal about Teenies once, a long time ago, when Bill was just a kit. Bogie had said that once there had been a great many Teenies in the world, and that it was a pity they were getting so thin... No cat ate anything better than a Teeny." When Bill had enquired of his grandfather at the pet shop where he was born and sold to the Wentworth family, if Teenies were "Leper-Cons," Bogie denied it: "That story was made up by dogs, and passed on, I'm sorry to say, by cats almost as stupid as they are... The word is even wrong... The right one is Leprechauns. Leprechauns are small creatures—creatures, not Humes or animals—that are supposed to live on the other side of the big water the Humes call the Ocean." Amongst the rumors Bogie had heard about Leprechauns is that "Old Man Splitfoot lets the leprechauns live forever if they will steal a Hume baby and replace it with a troll-baby..."

Just before Phil intervened to rescue him Sundance took the opportunity to dart forward and grab on to the cat's lower chest, which made Bill furious: "You have to understand this...the reason other animals regard Humes and Siamese with more fear and caution than they do any others...is because...they are the only animals that sometimes go mad." Another great King observation!

While trying to determine whether the little man was dead or alive Phil remembered his Poppa's funeral—when he thought he could see the dead man's chest rising and falling. When he raised this with his mother she opined that was because he wanted his grandfather to be alive. Phil said that wasn't it: "All of a sudden, Phil thought he knew why kids had to turn into grown-ups. It was because if you stayed a kid forever, the grown-ups would eventually drive you crazy with their stupid ideas and their deaf ears. He guessed that in

Reading the Lost Works of Stephen King

the end you turned into a grown-up in simple self-defense." Again, King at his finest.

Phil and Sundance is clearly another attempt at the storyline King was working on in *The Leprechaun*, which has been dated to around 1983, four years earlier. In that story (covered in *The Leprechaun* chapter of *Stephen King: Uncollected, Unpublished*) it is Owen King who interrupts *his* sister's cat (this time named Springsteen) tormenting something on the lawn, a "*...person,* a tiny little man wearing a green hat made out of a leaf. The little man looked back over his shoulder, and Owen saw how scared the little guy was."

The struggle between a little man-like creature and a cat also forms the basis of the screenplay *General* and a segment of the related movie script *Cat's Eye*, although the roles are reversed in that tale, with the cat being the hero. Those pieces were written around 1984, before King attempted and abandoned *Phil and Sundance* but with this new manuscript we have further evidence that King was fascinated with the relationship between cats and children (also a key plot device in *Pet Sematary*, which King first wrote in 1979).

•••

There are a number of satisfying links in the manuscript to King's other fiction (King's family calls these references "Easter Eggs"). With a Derry setting this unpublished fragment is linked to other Derry tales. Derry also appears in "Autopsy Room Four," *Bag of Bones*, "The Bird and the Album," *Dreamcatcher*, *11/22/63*, *Insomnia*, *It*, "The Road Virus Heads North," "Secret Window, Secret Garden," and *The Tommyknockers*. It is also mentioned in "The Body," "Comb

Dump," *The Dark Half, The Dark Tower VII: The Dark Tower, Dolores Claiborne, Gerald's Game, Hearts in Atlantis,* "Mrs. Todd's Shortcut," *Pet Sematary,* "The Revelations of 'Becka Paulson," *The Running Man, Storm of the Century,* "Uncle Otto's Truck." A number of Derry fixtures from other books are also mentioned, including Derry High, the Derry Mall and Jackson Street, Kansas Street and Main Street.

Sword in the Darkness

The manuscript of the unpublished novel *Sword in the Darkness* is held in Box 1010 at the Special Collections Unit of the Raymond H. Fogler Library at the University of Maine, Orono. Written permission from King is required to access this work. Dated April 30, 1970 it contains 485 double-spaced typed pages and is on the order of 150,000 words. Fortunately, King allowed me to publish the most important chapter in *Stephen King: Uncollected, Unpublished* and readers can therefore discover one of King's most important lost works there.

King recalls writing *Sword in the Darkness* during his senior year at the University of Maine, in Section 14 of the second part of *On Writing*: "...back in my dorm room was my dirty little secret: the half-completed manuscript of a novel about a teenage gang's plan to start a race riot. They would use this for cover while ripping off two dozen loan-sharking operations and illegal drug-rings in the city of Harding, my fictional version of Detroit (I had never been within six hundred miles of Detroit, but I didn't let that stop or even slow me down). This novel, *Sword in the Darkness,* seemed very tawdry to me when compared to what my fellow students were trying to achieve; which is why, I suppose, I

Reading the Lost Works of Stephen King

never brought any of it to class for a critique. The fact that it was also better and somehow truer than all my poems about sexual yearning and post-adolescent angst only made things worse. The result was a four-month period in which I could write almost nothing at all."

In the novel a gang of crooks is planning a race riot as cover for a series of robberies in the mid-Western city of Harding. The death of Rita from a brain tumor and the subsequent suicide of her daughter Miriam, unwed and pregnant, shatter the Kalowski family. Son and brother, Arnie, tries to deal with the losses as well as his love life with girlfriend, Janet Cross and sometime lover, Kit Longtin. Meanwhile, Kit Longtin and a gang friend blackmail the Harding High School principal, her uncle Henry Coolidge, who is something of a sex fiend. Confused? That's part of King learning to organize a novel, in this case making the mistake of jamming too much action in too quickly.

Edie Rowsmith and John Edgars, teachers at Harding High, are slowly building a relationship despite the fact that Edie is at least two decades older. They also try to help Arnie Kalowski. Marcus Slade, a radical African American, is to speak in Harding on June 29, 1969. Webs McCullough, a psychopathic criminal, plans to start the race riot during Slade's visit and commit his robberies during the mayhem.

Slade arrives and McCullough's men start the riot through a series of violent acts. A massive fire breaks out as blacks and whites fight across the city. Cross is raped by an African American and seriously injured. McCullough's men successfully rob various businesses, then proceed to stash their loot at the High School. Coolidge is in his office and shoots one of the gang before being killed himself. Finally realizing the psychopathic nature of their leader one of the gang shoots McCullough and the survivors escape the city. Plenty of action and drama!

In the aftermath of the riot, Kalowski discovers Cross has died from injuries sustained during the rape and runs into the night. The next morning he agrees to meet with Rowsmith and Edgars who now appear to have formed a more permanent relationship.

Chapter Seventy One is the most powerful section of the entire novel and would make a superb stand-alone story, subject to some rewriting and editing by King. Failing that, as mentioned, King allowed me to include it in *Stephen King: Uncollected, Unpublished*. It relates Edie Rowsmith's backstory in Gates Falls, Maine, before the Second World War. In reading this Chapter I formed the view that as a stand-alone effort it would represent one of the top ten or so of King's short stories. If a reader did not know this was King's writing from 1970 most would assume it was from a later King period, most likely the early 1980s. This makes it some of the most exciting of the material at the Fogler, a clear if slightly unpolished view of Stephen King the young professional writer. Indeed it makes it clear that King was destined to be a writer of the horrors humanity inflicts upon itself as much as mainstream horror, and most certainly not the standard run-of-the-mill writer of race riot and "contemporary" novels.

Edie Rowsmith's backstory is as poignant as any King has ever produced. She relates it to her school teacher friend and lover, John Edgars, the night of the Harding riots. Edie was one of twelve children, only four of whom lived beyond the age of five. She attended Gorham Normal School before moving to Gates Falls, Maine, in 1938, where she began teaching at a two-room school. She boarded with the Knowles family and she and the son, Donald, fell in love. Don was college educated, worked at a bank in Brunswick, and in addition to being the apple of his mother's eye was also the focus of her ambitions. When Don returned to Gates Falls with an engagement ring and told his mother, Cass Knowles he wanted to marry Edie she killed him with a kindling hatchet and cut off his genitals. Edie found the body later that morning, along with a catatonic Cass Knowles. Cass ended up in a "place" in Augusta (clearly Juniper Hill Asylum, which appears in many a King story). Her dreams lost, Edie moved to Harding and Edgars was the first chance she'd had for real love in the intervening thirty years.

One of the more interesting characters is "Webs" (short for "Cobwebs") McCullough, a psychopath in the tradition of *The Dead Zone*'s Greg Stillson. A white man, at an early age he began to kill cats and dogs. Aged fourteen, he killed a nine-year-old boy with a piece of rusty pipe. He left home at 15 and five years later turned up in Harding, where he revamped a local gang, the Oligarchs. In between he had killed an itinerant laborer in south Texas and an old woman in Reno. It was he who planned and started the riots in Harding.

Although it will never be published, *Sword and the Darkness* represents the debut of a famous King town—Gates Falls, Maine. Edie Rowsmith lived there with John and Cass Knowles before his mother murdered John, and Edie moved to Harding. Gates Falls is one of King's earliest towns and he has continued to mention it throughout his career. It is a key location in "Graveyard Shift," "It Grows on You," "The Revenge of Lard Ass Hogan," and "Riding the Bullet." It is also mentioned in *Blaze*, "The Body," *The Dark Half*, *The Dead Zone*, "Gramma," *Hearts in Atlantis*, "Movie Show" (an unpublished story fragment), "Mrs. Todd's Shortcut," *Needful Things*, *The Plant* (the electronic version only), *Rage* and *'Salem's Lot*. The town of Gates Center is mentioned and it also appears in "It Grows on You."

Harding, based on Detroit as noted earlier, appears to be the same city in which Richards lived in the Bachman novel, *The Running Man*. Richard Bachman is, of course, a King pseudonym.

As one of King's earliest attempts at a novel, *Sword in the Darkness* has numerous weaknesses, not the least of which is its overcomplicated, schizophrenic nature. There are simply too many storylines competing for the reader's attention, many of which add nothing to the overall impact. On the other hand it is exciting to see King bursting from the cocoon of his youth and college career, only three years before *Carrie* would be accepted for publication. Many of King's trademarks are clearly evident and future researchers will perhaps use this manuscript as a benchmark in King's career—one of the last transitional works before he became a fully-fledged brand-name author.

Another major flaw in the novel is the multitude of characters, which tend to overwhelm the reader and make it hard to keep all in focus. The gang members in particular go by a series of complicated nicknames and their gangs are hard to keep apart. The reader may also find it unclear which groups and characters are white and which black, something of a problem in a race riot novel. On the positive side King does a great job of showing the motivations of almost every character, a skill he would quickly refine.

The story has a Bachman flavor to it, with its dark, unrelenting spin deeper and deeper into disaster. This Bachman feel is not unexpected, considering a number of the novels later published as Bachman paperback originals were written very early in King's career.

The Cannibals

King originally attempted to write *The Cannibals* in 1978. His second attempt was a novel of about 450 pages, composed as a rewrite of an earlier novel written while filming *Creepshow* in July to December 1981. King wrote this in a footnote to his "Full Disclosure" in *Blaze*: "In my career I have managed to lose not one but two pretty good novels-in-progress. *Under the Dome* was only 50 pages long at the time it disappeared, but *The Cannibals* was over 200 pages long at the time it went MIA. No copies of either. That was before computers, and I never used carbons for first drafts—it felt *haughty*, somehow." King's assistant, Marsha DeFilippo indicated in posts on his official message board in April 2008 that, "We had sections, but not the complete draft, of *The Cannibals* in the office." As part of promoting *Under the Dome,* King released the first 61 pages of the second manuscript on his official website on September 15, 2009; and a further 63 pages on October 4th the same year—they may be read here: http://www.stephenking.com/library/unpublished/cannibals_the.html.

In June 2008, after an announcement King was writing *Under the Dome,* DeFilippo reported on the official message board King saying: "Those stories were two very different attempts to utilize the same idea, which concerns itself with how people behave when they are cut off from the society they've always belonged to. Also, my memory of THE CANNIBALS is that it, like NEEDFUL THINGS, was a kind of social comedy. The new UNDER THE DOME is played dead straight." Bear in mind also that *The Cannibals* was attempted between 1978 and 1981, *Under the Dome* more than a quarter century later.

The first section, a scan of King's original typewritten manuscript, with handwritten corrections, is comprised of the first three chapters and the first two subsections of the fourth chapter from Part One of the novel.

Part One is titled "Yellow Morning" (in King's handwriting, crossing out three other words) and Chapter I is "The Tennis Club." We are introduced to the Tennis Club Apartments, whose residents are immediately portrayed as isolated from general society—upper middle-class, white collar people "who lived mostly for themselves in the era of withdrawal from commitment" (the story is set at some point in the 1980s, when "Greed is Good" was a mantra, and conspicuous consumption was all the rage, especially with DINK—"Double Income No Kids"—households).

Chapter II is "Tom Hill in the Lobby" and features the first resident "to encounter the problem which arose on July 19th." A TV station executive on the way up, Hill is heading to work around 4:45 AM and proceeds to the apartment building's foyer and pulls on the outer door, which does not open, in fact when he pulls the door again it doesn't budge even slightly. Hill notices the approaching daylight is more suited to one hour later in the morning (a nice piece of foreshadowing). Only slightly irritated and investigating, Hill finds the building phone is not working and decides to head upstairs.

Reading the Lost Works of Stephen King

In Chapter III—"Pulaski"—another character is introduced, arriving in the lobby just as Hill headed back up in the elevator. We learn Dennis Pulaski is a twice-divorced Korean War veteran, a hunter and something of a "man's man." This section contains quite a bit of sexual content, mostly designed to establish the rigidity of Pulaski's worldview. He's also a racist. Pulaski discovers he too is unable to open the building's front door. He is perhaps the Big Jim Rennie of the piece.

Meanwhile, Hill knocks on the building office door, looking for Ronnie Bamford, the night security guard. But there's no answer. Returning downstairs, he meets Pulaski, who informs him the back doors are also locked. They consider exiting through the alarmed fire door, which leads to the nearby sports complex but when they try, "The square of metal did not move at all. It did not move an inch, a half-inch, not so much as a silly millimeter. The alarm did not sound. And the fire door did not open." This disturbs the two men, who understand that locking a normal door is one thing, locking a fire escape is serious indeed.

When they return to the lobby, quite a few more residents have appeared and are milling about. Pulaski rings the building superintendent, Rinaldi, and demands he come downstairs immediately. We learn that Rinaldi is a pompous control freak and not easily intimidated. As the residents wait for the superintendent to appear, Pulaski also notes the daylight, he "could not remember ever having seen daylight quite like this one—thin, watery, almost *wavery*." Rinaldi finally appears and also tries to leave the building. When he cannot it is revealed the external doors *cannot* be locked, as in fact they *have no locks*.

Chapter IV is "Jo's Bible; Rinaldi's Call; Pulaski's Bat" and begins with another in the growing cast of characters—a deeply religious Joanne Page. By the time she reaches the lobby, Rinaldi, Hill and Pulaski have left for Rinaldi's office. Rinaldi's jaundiced, perhaps realistic view of the building's occupants is revealed—they are each classified in his mind as Busybodies, Good Tenants, or Troublemakers. Careful to preserve his authority with the residents, and mindful of not looking incompetent to his employers, Rinaldi begins by calling the security guard's company on a dedicated line, but not before the first of likely many clashes with Pulaski. The security company answers and Rinaldi can hear the operator, Bo Franklin, but Franklin most certainly cannot hear Rinaldi. The three men begin to show concern, in Tom Hill's case, "he felt something pierce his confusion and harried annoyance at being late. He found nothing welcome about the new emotion. It was fear." And so ends the first manuscript segment.

The second section is also a scan of King's original typewritten manuscript, with handwritten corrections. It continues directly from the first section and is comprised of the remainder of the fourth chapter and part of chapter five.

As the story continues we learn more of Jo Page's peculiarly individual religious fervor—she is happy to study the Bible but won't attend church. She also notices the light, which frightens her, "She'd never seen daylight of that particular sick quality; had never, in fact, seen an artificial light which was quite like it." Looking at it, "she felt her insides go cold and numb. Her fingers and toes momentarily lost all sense of feeling, and for a horrifying space of time—perhaps only a second or two; however long it was, it seemed much longer in her mind—she was afraid she was going to wet herself."

Pulaski insists Rinaldi recognize there is a real problem, while the superintendent seeks to maintain his dwindling authority. More people are gathering in the lobby and they are also beginning to notice the strange nature of the light, through which "the cars in the parking lot stood out like pop-ups in a child's activity book. They looked so real that they somehow went too far and seemed false." The residents notice there is no traffic on the nearby Interstate highway, which at this commuting hour is impossible. When Jo looks that way she momentarily sees traffic, which disappears with next blink of her eyelids. After deliberately squeezing her eyes shut, the traffic returns and stays.

The superintendent and the two tenants move to Rinaldi's apartment, only to find the same problem with a normal telephone line—they can call out but no one can hear them. When Hill calls the television station another weird event occurs—the sound of the receptionist's voice suddenly "accelerated so rapidly that it became insectile, unintelligible…the hideous thing was somehow *organic*…" At this point the story has a Lovecraftian feel.

Back in the foyer some of the residents are losing it—one man is chanting, "The cars are there" over and over. As they watch the traffic appears and disappears, then reappears. Pulaski returns to his apartment, where he is revealed as something of a gun fanatic, but ignores the firearms and instead grabs a baseball bat. More of Pulaski's backstory is revealed, including how he had survived what he thought was certain death in a robbery when he was driving a taxi. After that scare he started carrying the bat in his cab, and had used it when another robbery was attempted—"the junkie didn't wake up for four days, and Pulaski heard he didn't walk right for six weeks. Pulaski didn't lose any sleep over it."

Hill is already back in the foyer when Pulaski returns with his bat, and his appearance immediately inspires both fear and respect among the milling residents. Pulaski intends to smash the foyer glass but when he strikes it with full force it not only doesn't smash, it doesn't "so much as shiver." Real concern sweeps the crowd.

Chapter V is titled "The Tennis Club (II); First Weird Scenes inside the Goldmine." It's now 8:00 AM and almost all the residents are both awake and realize a serious problem has developed. Another group of residents forms and converge upon Rinaldi's apartment, demanding answers and that he give them the keys to the doors that form the normal entryways to the Tennis Club.

As matters begin to spiral out of control Tom Hill observes "scenes both comic and tragic" that he comes to think of as "weird scenes inside the goldmine." The term would come into common use by those trapped inside the building and had been coined by Jo Page, who'd remembered a line from "The End" by The Doors. These "scenes" introduce more characters and we learn the building has no television or radio reception (further isolating the residents), and that the world is receding further (now the leaves on nearby trees are sometimes visible, sometimes not). Some take to booze, others to drugs. The story starts to meander at this point and the segment ends.

It seems unlikely King will release more of the manuscript, as to do that after nearly a quarter of the unpublished work was publicly available would be tantamount to full publication of an unedited and incomplete novel. We can presume many of the social issues of isolation in a limited society are dealt with in *Under the Dome* and we will most likely never know what phenomenon is responsible for the isolation of the apartment building. The most compelling part of what we can read is the strangeness of the outside world and, while there are the beginnings of interesting characterizations, they do seem a little one-dimensional. Of course, we are left to contemplate the meaning of the novel's title.

These three examples give a taste of what hidden King works there are for readers. These are the best part of a hundred partial or complete works either unpublished or not included in one of King's fiction collections. Avid readers will have little problem accessing many, or at least a good description of them, in *Stephen King: Uncollected, Unpublished* and elsewhere.

So, as we discovered at the beginning of this essay, the benefits of searching out and reading "lost" Stephen King works are: an understanding of how King developed as a writer; an understanding of the similarities and dissimilarities in these obscure works to his better known canon; and, as always with King, the pure joy of reading a King story for the first or, for that matter, nineteenth time!

In other words, great reward for effort. Happy reading!

Twins and Twinning in Stephen King's Dark Tower Novels

ROBIN FURTH

Spoilers Warning: This article contains information about the last Dark Tower novels.

Human beings have always been fascinated by twins. In mythologies from the ancient Near East to the Mediterranean, Africa, and the Americas, stories of divine twins abound.

Whether they are allied siblings, rival brothers, or twin-soul lovers, mythic twins are two halves of a whole. In almost all stories, mythic twins are polarized. Their natures remind us of the duality of the perceived universe: heaven and earth, light and dark, life and death, male and female, divine and mortal, good and evil.[2] To modern readers versed in psychology, the twin is often a symbol of the shadow self, a kind of doppelganger that manifests our repressed desires and emotions. In contemporary science, twinning has taken on yet

---

2 To read more about the mythic roots of twins and twinning, see Brian Clark's article, "The Twin Motif in Comparative Mythology," listed in the bibliography.

another meaning. According to the Many Worlds Theory of quantum physics, there are an infinite number of alternate earths that exist in the same space and time as our own, and though we can never travel to these twin worlds, other versions of us are living out their lives in these parallel realities.[3] According to the Many Worlds Theory, time is not linear but more closely resembles a branching tree. Each time we make a decision, the time/space continuum splits to encompass each possible outcome, and new worlds are born.

For Stephen King's Constant Readers, the concept of multiple worlds and multiple selves is a familiar one. Twins and twinners, parallel realities and monstrous doubles are some of Stephen King's most enduring motifs. In King's creative universe, all forms of twinning can be found. In *The Dark Half*, the author Thad Beaumont discovers that he has literally split into two people, his conscious self—a university professor and acclaimed literary novelist—and the dark, unsavory character of his pseudonym—the murderous and vengeful George Stark. In the novel *Desperation*, people who are taken over by the demonic entity Tak transform into infernal, larger-than-life, murderous versions of themselves. And in *The Talisman* and *Black House* (co-written with Peter Straub), people in our world have twinners, or doubles, in a parallel, medieval world known as the Territories. In Stephen King's universe, as in the Multiple Worlds Theory, time is not linear. Alternate earths and parallel worlds coexist, and although they are invisible to us, we are surrounded by them. The difference between Stephen King's imaginative universe and the Multiple Worlds theory is that, in King's multiverse, all worlds are connected

---

[3] For more information, see Lev Vaidman's article, "Many-Worlds Interpretation of Quantum Mechanics," listed in the bibliography.

Twins and Twinning in Stephen King's Dark Tower Novels

by a single nexus in the time/space continuum. As Constant Readers know very well, that nexus point where all worlds meet is known as the Dark Tower.

In the afterword of *Wizard and Glass*, which is Book IV of the Dark Tower series, Stephen King writes, "I have written enough novels and short stories to fill a solar system of the imagination, but Roland's story is my Jupiter—a planet that dwarfs all others" (671). According to King, Roland's world (or worlds) actually contains all others of his making. It is, in essence, the heart of his creative universe. It also holds the key to King's fascination with the literary motif of twins and twinning.

I. Roland Deschain, the Dark Tower, and the importance of Twinning to the Quest

Written over a period of almost forty years and consisting of eight novels and one novella, Stephen King's Dark Tower series spans the length of his prolific literary career. It tells the story of Roland Deschain, a wandering gunslinger-knight in a land called Mid-World. Due to the poisonous fallout of the wars waged by Mid-World's Great Old Ones (a technologically advanced but brutal people), as well as the civil wars that ravaged the landscape and decimated the populace during Roland's youth, Mid-World has become a poisoned wasteland. As the final descendant of Arthur Eld, the ancient King of All-World, Roland's fate is bound to the fate of his land, and its ruin or redemption is tied to his own. Because of this, Roland is on a quest. His goal is to find the Dark Tower, which is the linchpin of the time/space continuum, and to climb to the top to question whatever god or demon resides there. It is also to defeat the Crimson King and his Beam Breakers who are using their psychic powers to erode the magnetic Beams that hold the Tower in place. Roland hopes that if he reaches the Tower, he will be able to both regenerate his world and redeem his own soul, but the path to redemption is far from easy.

Over the course of Roland's long trek, we begin to realize that there are actually two Rolands: the accomplished and highly trained killer, and the just and fair-minded descendant of kings. Unbeknownst to Roland, his journey is not a linear one but a repeating loop. He has not traveled to the Tower once but many times, and in each journey, the balance between killer and king shifts a little more towards the "White" or the good. Roland needs his gunslinger's instincts to survive, but as the skills of the gunman become secondary to the consciousness and moral order of the king, Roland's ultimate redemption, and Mid-World's rejuvenation, comes a little closer. Whether Roland's many journeys exist in one world or in multiple, parallel worlds, we do not know. But what we begin to realize is that Roland's quest is not just about saving Mid-World. Roland's world and our world are twins, and the terrible ruin that Roland's world has experienced is one possible fate of our own. Only if Roland protects the Dark Tower can both our world, and Mid-World, be saved.

In Greek mythology, twins often appear in narratives where there is a striving towards consciousness, order, and the rule of law.[4] Divine twins are associated with healing, reviving the dead, increasing fertility, and ensuring victory in

---

4 See Brian Clark's "The Twin Motif in Comparative Mythology," listed in the bibliography.

Twins and Twinning in Stephen King's Dark Tower Novels

battle. Since these are the very purposes of Roland's quest—to heal Mid-World and to restore fertility and order to the land—King's use of the twin motif gives his story a powerful mythological resonance. But King's use of the twin has a profound psychological significance as well. Many of the characters Roland meets over the course of his journey are internally divided between a conscious self and a shadow self. One of Roland's tests during his travels is whether he can help these fragmented beings integrate their many selves and become whole. Those who integrate become companions. Those who do not, either obliterate themselves or are sacrificed for the sake of the quest.

Another influence upon the twinning found in the Dark Tower novels is the concept of *ka*. Like many words in High Speech, which is the ancient language of Mid-World's gunslinger elite, ka has multiple meanings. It signifies life force, consciousness, duty or destiny. In the vulgate, or low speech, it also means a place to which an individual must go. The closest terms in our language are probably *fate* and *destiny*, although ka also implies karma, or the accumulated destiny and debt, of many existences. We are the servants of ka, but we are also its prisoners. Ka is the root of many High Speech terms, such as *ka-tet* (a group bound by fate and destiny), *ka-dinh* (leader), and *ka-mai* (destiny's fool). Unlike destiny, ka does not reveal itself along a linear timeline. Often referred to as a wheel, it is seen as circular. As they say in Mid-World, "ka [is] a wheel, its one purpose to turn, and in the end it always [comes] back to the place where it had started" (*Waste Lands*, 394). Because of ka, situations, places, and even people (or their doubles) are encountered again and again over the course of a life. Many of the twins and doubles that Roland encounters on his journey seem to emphasize the cyclical nature of *ka*.

II: Polarized Twins and the Shadow Self: Odetta Holmes and Detta Walker

The first time that twins and twinning are explored at length in the Dark Tower series is in Book II, *The Drawing of the Three*, and its importance is both personal and political. The Civil Rights Movement and African-Americans' fight for equality is one that King often touches upon in his fiction, so it is not surprising that the subject arises in the Dark Tower series. In *The Drawing of the Three* we meet Odetta Holmes, a wealthy, intelligent, and beautiful African-American woman living in New York City during the Civil Rights Era. Born Odetta Susannah Holmes, daughter of the dentist/inventor Dan Holmes and heir to his vast fortune, Odetta is an educated and socially aware individual, a vocal Civil Rights advocate pressing the United States to become a more equal and just nation. But the open-minded, egalitarian Odetta Holmes has a shadow side, a secret self she is not aware of. That self is an angry, street-wise woman named Detta Walker.

Odetta's second personality, that of Detta Walker, was born when Odetta was hit on the head with a brick when she was five years old. This accident took place in Elizabeth, New Jersey, during the 1940s.[5] By this time Odetta's father was already becoming a wealthy man, thanks to his patented dental capping process, but his wealth could not protect

---

[5] Since Odetta was brought to Mid-World in the early 1960s and she was already at least twenty-six years old, she must have been five years old sometime during the 1940s.

Twins and Twinning in Stephen King's Dark Tower Novels

his family against Jim Crow, or the endemic racism of the Southern United States.

Jim Crow—a name taken from a nineteenth century minstrel show character that caricatured African-American slaves—was the term used to describe a series of laws that legalized a Southern caste system based on race. Its underlying doctrine—born out of the racism used to justify slavery—was that African-American people were inferior to Caucasians and thus could be treated as second-class citizens. In all its myriad forms, Jim Crow was demeaning and humiliating. It meant that black passengers traveling on Southern trains were barred from using any amenities, from the "white only" toilets, water fountains, and dining cars, to the "white only" sleeper cars. (No alternate facilities were offered.) Jim Crow meant that waiting rooms were segregated, and that white travelers buying tickets always took priority.

Ironically, it was during a trip from the South (where segregation was still practiced) to the North (where it was not), that five-year-old Odetta seems to have first become aware of the hardships suffered by people of color in America, an awareness that ultimately gave birth to Detta. In order to attend her maternal aunt's marriage ceremony in New Jersey, Odetta and her parents made the trip North in the segregated Jim Crow Car. As an African-American child living in the Southern states, Odetta would have experienced the unfairness of Jim Crow laws already. But it was this particular confrontation with the unfairness of Jim Crow (in conjunction with the head injury that Odetta suffered soon after) that crystalized not only Odetta's awareness of race issues in America but also focused the unconscious rage which gave birth to the angry personality of Detta Walker.

Confrontation with the unfairness of Jim Crow was not the only shock that five-year-old Odetta had to deal with during this trip North. Near the end of their visit, the Holmes family faced yet another racially-based humiliation, showing young Odetta that it was not only the South where racism was prevalent. The day after Blue's wedding, a taxi driver refused to give Odetta and her parents a ride to the train station because he did not want an African-American family in his cab. In order to avoid the embarrassment of being refused by yet another taxi driver, the Holmes family decided to walk to the station. On the way, a white sociopath named Jack Mort, waiting in a nearby derelict building, dropped a brick on young Odetta's head, catapulting Odetta into a three-week-long coma. (Interestingly, Mort also suffered from a type of split personality disorder. By profession he was a successful accountant, but his hobby was killing, or "depth-charging" people [321].)

Although the police declared that Odetta's injury was an accident, Odetta's parents secretly believed that the incident had been a racist hate-crime. So did Odetta. Although this coma served as Detta's gestation period, this secondary personality did not have much waking time until about twenty years later, when Jack Mort once again entered Odetta's life. This time, Mort pushed Odetta in front of an A train, severing her legs from the knee down. After this horrific accident, Detta gained more and more waking time.

Given the tragedies of her personal history and the racism that had shaped her experience, it is not surprising that Odetta's suppressed rage laid the foundations for the secondary personality of Detta Walker, a woman who boiled over with the frustration, rage, and vengefulness that Odetta

Twins and Twinning in Stephen King's Dark Tower Novels

Holmes could not consciously admit. Odetta's psyche was divided, but so was the United States that she knew. Odetta was a wealthy African-American woman born into a world where the Supreme Court's 1896 *Plessy vs. Ferguson*'s ruling—that racial separation was allowable—had not yet been successfully challenged. Odetta/Detta was injured and disabled, but her injury and disablement mirrored the legal and social injustices inflicted upon African-American people, and the "disablement" of their civil rights, which the law had upheld.

In Detta, Odetta manifests everything her Christian parents and careful upbringing had made her suppress. Whereas Odetta was soft-spoken, Detta was outrageously outspoken. Whereas Odetta believed in using legal action against bigotry, Detta took a more personal and direct approach, namely outraging white society whenever possible. However, Detta was not immune to emotional transference. Instead of raging against the man who dropped a brick on her head, or against the police force that did not investigate the crime properly, Detta blamed Odetta's Aunt Blue for her injury. One of the memories that would later trigger her switch from Odetta to Detta was the recollection of the blue and white "forspecial" plate that Odetta's parents gave to Blue as her wedding gift [393]. One of Detta's first acts as a separate self was to steal and destroy this plate.

Although some of Detta's actions may seem shocking to contemporary readers, once her rage is placed in a social and historical context, it is understandably human. After all, it is the rage any individual feels under the yoke of oppression. It is not until Roland Deschain forces Odetta and Detta to confront each other's existence—and Odetta's morality and social awareness are brought into conscious co-existence with Detta's rage—that the two conflicting personalities can unite into the much stronger third of Susannah Holmes, who soon becomes Susannah Dean, wife of Eddie Dean, a young man from New York 1987 whom Roland has already drawn into Mid-World to take part in his quest.

Although Odetta and Detta join and become part of a unified whole, Susannah is not yet finished with twinning. In *The Wolves of the Calla*, we discover that Susannah Dean has developed yet another twin, or (as they say in High Speech) *twim*. This twin is Mia, which in High Speech means *mother*. Unlike Susannah's previous dual personalities of Odetta Holmes/Detta Walker, Mia is not generated by a deep psychological schism within her host. Originally Mia was one of the disincarnate spirits left behind on Mid-World's shores when the magical Prim receded. However, Mia gave up her immortality to hijack Susannah Dean's body and bear a child. The child that Susannah-Mia conceives in the haunted Speaking Ring on the road to Lud is the child of two fathers (Roland Deschain and The Crimson King) and two mothers (Susannah herself and Mia, daughter of none). This child is known as Mordred Red-Heel, and according to prophecy, he is destined to be Roland's killer.

As someone who has suffered from multiple personality disorder/dissociative identity disorder, Susannah recognizes the fact that Mid-World itself is "a world of twins and mirror images," and that the child she and Mia conceive in the supernatural Speaking Ring is no exception (*Dark Tower*, 76). Like so many of the divine twins of legend who are both mortal and immortal, good and evil, Mordred is eternally divided. As Susannah muses, "Mordred too was a twin, a

Twins and Twinning in Stephen King's Dark Tower Novels

Jekyll and Hyde creature with two selves, and he—or it—had the faces of two fathers to remember" (76).

By nature, Mordred is a were-spider. His human body is like that of his human "White Daddy" Roland (*Dark Tower*, 620), but his arachnid body conforms to the nature of his immortal "Red Daddy," the Crimson King (76). Mordred's hungers, however, seem to come from his Red Daddy. Not long after being born, Mordred transforms into his spider shape and devours his birth-mother, Mia. Ultimately, Mordred dies without fulfilling his destiny. Instead of killing Roland, Mordred dies from eating poisoned meat.

III. North Central Positronics and the Twin Natures of Technology

In *The Waste Lands* (Book III of the Dark Tower cycle), Roland and his ka-tet travel to the ancient metropolis of Lud where they meet Blaine, yet another being with split personality disorder. But unlike Susannah Dean, Blaine isn't human. Although Blaine's identity focuses on the bubblegum-pink monorail located in the Cradle of Lud (the city's equivalent of a train station), he is, by his own admission, much more than this. He is the city's central computer, controlling the automated systems of the once thriving metropolis, from its ventilation systems and transportation system to its defensive weapons. Like so many of North Central Positronics creations, Blaine runs on slo-trans technology, a technology that is supposed to be immune to equipment malfunction. But as proves to be the case with NCP's other Artificial Intelligences that we meet later in the series, Blaine is fragmenting. According to the

Pubes—one of the two rival gangs warring for control of the ruined city—Blaine is the most dangerous of all the ghosts that live in the city's machines, ghosts that bear only ill-will to humans (232-33). But in truth, Blaine is *all* of the ghosts in the machines, and he is even more dangerous than the Pubes realize.

Just as Lud's population is divided between the warring gangs of the Pubes and the Grays, Blaine the computer has fragmented into several opposed personalities. The dominant personality is that of Blaine the Mono. Both cruel and unpredictable, Blaine is completely insane. As he tells Roland's ka-tet, he has decided that he serves the people of Lud best by acting as their erratic and fickle god:

AT SOME POINT THEY FORGOT THAT THE VOICE OF THE MONO WAS ALSO THE VOICE OF THE COMPUTER. NOT LONG AFTER THAT THEY FORGOT I WAS A SERVANT AND BEGAN BELIEVING I WAS A GOD. SINCE I WAS BUILT TO SERVE, I FULFILLED THEIR REQUIREMENTS AND BECAME WHAT THEY WANTED—A GOD DISPENSING BOTH FAVOR AND PUNISHMENT ACCORDING TO WHIM...(410).

In Lud, Blaine runs the god-drums that drive the Pubes to sacrifice one of their number every day. (They believe that if they do not appease the god-drums, the ghosts in the machines will animate the dead and rise up to eat the living.) He also kills those who visited him in his cradle by electrocuting them with blue fire. After Roland and his travelling companions board Blaine to leave for his final destination of Topeka, Blaine kills all of the city's remaining inhabitants with poison gas. He also threatens to kill Roland's ka-tet unless they can beat him in a riddling contest.

Twins and Twinning in Stephen King's Dark Tower Novels

By the time Roland meets Blaine, one of his secondary personalities (that of his "companion" Patricia) is already dead. While still functioning, Patricia was Blaine's twin monorail. Like the opposing twins of folklore, Patricia was blue to Blaine's pink, female to his male, and traveling northwest to his southeast. While Blaine is the computer's sadistic mind, Patricia was the computer's (now dead) emotional center. According to Blaine, Patricia went mad after the fall of the city. She sobbed constantly, in part due to a spiritual malaise, in part because of loneliness. Rather than let her "logic faults" spread to the rest of the computer system, Blaine isolated the problem and erased all circuits controlling Patricia's non-voluntaries. Patricia responded by throwing herself into the river. Although Blaine sees himself as separate from Patricia, he admits that (like Patricia before him) he is also suffering from "a spiritual malaise beyond [his] ability to repair," and is going both senile and insane (410).

Big Blaine is a psychotic bully and the deceased Patricia was a sobbing suicidal wreck, but Blaine's third personality plays a very different role in the computer's sense of self. Little Blaine, as this aspect calls himself, is the last part of the computer's fragmented personality that remembers it was originally designed to serve and not to destroy. When Roland and his ka-tet finally enter Blaine for their trip southeast, they get a sense of what the unified Blaine once was. The voice that welcomes them onto the train is a version of Little Blaine. But unlike the terrified whisper that Eddie and Susannah hear when they first try to wake the Mono, this voice is soothing and confident. Little Blaine must have also originally been allied with the White or the good, since when he speaks his intercom glows with a rosy pink light, as opposed to Big Blaine, who makes the intercom glow an angry red.

Although Big Blaine is unaware of Little Blaine, Little Blaine knows all too well the dangers of interacting with Big Blaine. Eddie and Susannah describe Little Blaine's voice as that of "a child who has lived with [a] psychotic adult for a long time, hiding in corners and stealing out only when it knows the adult is asleep" (347). As he says of himself, *"I'm Little Blaine... The one he doesn't see. The one he forgot. The one he thinks he left behind in the rooms of ruin and the halls of the dead"* (347). Whenever possible, Little Blaine whispers out of a single speaker, so as to remain hidden from the computer's larger, insane consciousness. Little Blaine knows that if Big Blaine becomes aware of his existence, he will destroy him as he destroyed Patricia. As he says when Eddie and Susannah rouse Big Blaine from his sleep, *"I can't let him catch me! I can't let him kill me too!"* (348).

Throughout their time with Big Blaine, Little Blaine is the voice that warns them against Big Blaine's unpredictability and dangerousness. His advice is always the same: run and hide, and if you can't, appease Big Blaine at any cost. Unfortunately for Little Blaine, Big Blaine never manages to reunite with his fragmented parts. Instead, his circuits are fried by Eddie's silly riddles and Blaine—now mindless—crashes into his termination point of Topeka.

IV: The Twins of Calla Bryn Sturgis

In *The Wolves of the Calla*, the motif of the twin moves from the psychological realm to that of the physical. In Calla Bryn Sturgis, a village located in Mid-World's Borderlands,

Twins and Twinning in Stephen King's Dark Tower Novels

twins are the norm and singletons—or children born without a twin—are rarities. But there is a sinister twist to this birthing anomaly. Once each generation, a band of masked riders known as Wolves gallops out of the dark land of Thunderclap to steal one of every set of prepubescent twins born in the Callas. The children are taken to Thunderclap so that the Crimson King's servants can cull the enzyme in their brains that causes twin-telepathy. This enzyme is then fed to the Beam Breakers in End-World to enhance their Beam-Breaking abilities.

When the children are finally returned to the Calla, they are mentally and physically ruined, or roont. No matter how clever they were before being taken, once they return, their intellectual capabilities are not much more than those of infants. Few can do manual labor and even fewer can speak. The roonts remain childlike until about the age of sixteen, when they grow to an enormous size. This growing process happens extremely rapidly (within a year and a half they transform from small children to young giants) and is excruciatingly painful. But despite their size, roonts remain sexually dead and never procreate. When they reach their thirties, most grow shockingly old and die, often of a disease that looks like cancer. Their endings are rarely pain-free.

When Roland and his ka-tet arrive in Calla Bryn Sturgis, they are surprised by just how similar the Calla's sets of twins are, despite the fact that most are of opposite sexes, and so are fraternal rather than identical. The tragedy of this similarity soon becomes apparent. While one twin will grow up and become a valuable member of the Calla's small society, the other twin—though born equally attractive, intelligent, and capable—will become roont.

The poignancy of the Calla's devastated twins is illustrated by the response that a married couple (Zalia and Tian) have to their roont siblings:

•••

[Zalia] turned back to Tian. They looked at each other, a man and a woman not roont, but only because of dumb luck. So far as either of them knew, it could just as easily have been Zal and Tia standing in here and watching Tian and Zalia out by the barn, grown large of body and empty of head (11).

•••

Like all of the twins in the Calla, Tia and Tian, Zalia and Zalman, were almost identical children. Despite their different genders, we sense that in physical appearance and intelligence, they were equal. Seeing Zalman and Tia through Zalia and Tian's eyes, we gain not just sympathy for these unlucky giants, but empathy. They become a mirror for Zalia and Tian, and a mirror for us. Had fate made just a slightly different turn, Zal and Tia could have remained whole. Yet had fate twisted differently, who knows what tragedies might have unfolded in their world, or ours? We all know people who have had terrible accidents and have lost the ability to use parts of their bodies, or even parts of their intellects. And in the end, isn't it just luck that we have remained healthy? In this particular instance, twinning reminds us of the unfairness of ka, which has neither heart nor mind. As they say in Mid-World, "here we are, and ka stands to one side and laughs" (395).

Twins and Twinning in Stephen King's Dark Tower Novels

V. Twinning and Ka

In the Dark Tower novels the motif of twins and twinning has subtle resonances beyond the realms of the psychological, political, or even the physical. Sometimes, the image of the twin or double emphasizes the cyclical nature of ka, or fate, and the repeating elements of Roland's journey. Both Calla Bryn Sturgis (*The Wolves of the Calla*) and Hambry (*Wizard and Glass*) contain saloons called The Travelers' Rest, and the same honky-tonk piano player (Sheb) works in both Hambry's saloon and Tull's (*The Gunslinger*). While in Hambry, Roland meets Francis Lengyll, President of the corrupt Horsemen's Association and owner of the Rocking B Ranch. While in Calla Bryn Sturgis, Roland meets Vaughn Eisenhart, an important rancher who *also* owns a ranch called the Rocking B. Although Eisenhart isn't corrupt, his foreman, Ben Slightman, is a traitor to the town.

Such twinning can also occur between worlds. For example, we are told that Roland's childhood friend and ka-mate Cuthbert Allgood (born in Mid-World) is the twinner of Eddie Dean (born in our world). Henchick, the dinh (or leader) of Manni Redpath near Calla Bryn Sturgis, is the twin of a crazed preacher from our world called Reverend Earl Harrigan. Father Callahan (a major character from King's novel *'Salem's Lot,* and later a priest in Calla Bryn Sturgis) is the twin of the ka-mate that Roland meets in End-World's Devar-Toi, Ted Brautigan. To further the link between Mid-World and all of King's other written works and worlds, we find out from Ted Brautigan that Roland's twelve-year-old ka-mate, Jake Chambers, is the double of Bobby Garfield (the main character of "Low Men in Yellow Coats"). Bryan

Smith, who hit Stephen King with his Dodge minivan both in the real world and in the Dark Tower series, is said to be the twin of Sheemie Ruiz, Roland's friend from Hambry whom he also meets in End-World's Devar-Toi. Even Bryan Smith's dogs, Bullet and Pistol, are litter-twins.

In Mid-World, ka decrees that the motif of the twin is built into the structure of the multiverse itself. As above, so below; as below, so above. According to the metaphysical map of Mid-World that Roland drew in *The Waste Lands*, Mid-World is shaped like a wheel. At the wheel's hub sits the Dark Tower, linchpin of the time/space continuum. Crossing at this nexus point are the six Beams, which simultaneously hold the Dark Tower in place and maintain the proper alignment of time, space, size, and dimension. Watching over each of these twelve termination points are twelve animal totems known as Guardians.

Like the kabbalistic Tree of Life found in our world, Mid-World's map has a darker side. Just as each Beam has two designated Guardians, each Beam is also overseen by the Guardians' dark twins, beings known as Demon Elementals. Although there are only six Demon Elementals, there are twelve demon aspects (one for each Guardian), since each demon has a male and female self. The Guardians of the Beam watch over the mortal world, but the hermaphroditic Demon Elementals watch over the invisible world of demons, ghosts, and ill-sicks. If the Guardians' original purpose was to serve the White, or the force of good, at least some of the Demon Elementals serve the Outer Dark. Just as the Turtle Guardian protects Roland and his tet on the way to the Tower, the Demon Elementals (who are in league with Roland's enemy, the Crimson King), are trying

Twins and Twinning in Stephen King's Dark Tower Novels

to thwart Roland's quest. In fact, it is the Demon Elementals who are central to the creation of Roland's ultimate nemesis: his half-son, Mordred.

VI. There are Other Worlds than These

At the end of *The Gunslinger*, Roland's eleven-year-old traveling companion, Jake Chambers, falls to his death beneath the Cyclopean Mountains. As Roland lets the boy tumble into the abyss (more intent upon following the Man in Black than on saving the life of his young comrade), Jake utters his famous lines, "Go then. There are other worlds than these" (revised edition, 205). No one knows about these other worlds better than Jake, since he was born in our world and only entered Roland's reality after dying in ours.

From the beginning of the Dark Tower series, Stephen King hints that Mid-World and our world are connected by more than just magical doorways. From the outset of *The Gunslinger*, we realize that Mid-World and our world are eerily similar. Not only does Roland's reality look like the nineteenth century American West, but the people there know about the Bible, and the "Man Jesus." They are familiar with Beatles songs such as "Hey Jude," and revere a mythical hero named Arthur Eld, who is very similar to our world's King Arthur. When Roland and Jake travel through the tunnels below the Cyclopean Mountains, Roland recalls a mad preacher whose followers worshipped a thunder god named after an Amoco gasoline pump. Under those same mountains, Roland and Jake follow train tracks to a subway station, where Roland can read some of the English signs which seem to him to be the ancient root of High Speech, the sacred language of gunslingers. But it is in *The Waste Lands* that we begin to suspect that Mid-World and our world are not just connected; they overlap.

When Blaine the Mono crashes into his (literal) termination point, Roland's tet finds itself in a place called Topeka, which is "the place where Mid-World end[s] and End-World beg[ins]" (*Waste Lands,* 420). But much to their surprise, our tet discovers that Mid-World's Topeka is very similar to the city of the same name found in our world. The sign at the terminal building reads, ATCHISON, TOPEKA, AND SANTA FE, the name of the railroad that once extended over much of the American West. After disembarking, they see signs for the Kansas Turnpike, and parking lots are full of familiar cars such as Chevrolets and Chryslers (if also the less familiar Takuro Spirits). Soft drinks in cans much like those produced by Coca-Cola are for sale (though here they are called Nozz-A-La). According to a newspaper they find, it is 1986, the year before Eddie Dean left our world, but unlike Eddie's 1986, in this one, the population has been wiped out by a virus called superflu.

As the novel progresses, these overlaps continue. While traveling through River Barony, our ka-tet discovers a downed airplane, which Jake identifies as a pre-World War II German Focke-Wülf, whose swastika insignia has been covered by a fist and thunderbolt design. When our tet reaches the city of Lud, they think that the bridge across the River Send looks remarkably like the George Washington Bridge leading to Manhattan. In fact, the more we learn about the Great Old Ones who built the ruined city of Lud, the more the ancestors of Roland's people look like our descendants.

Twins and Twinning in Stephen King's Dark Tower Novels

But as we learn in *The Wolves of the Calla,* our world and Mid-World are not the only realities to be closely linked. In flashback, Father Callahan tells us of his journey along the todash turnpikes of America. According to Callahan, these highways in hiding radiate out from New York "like a spider's web" (293). What Callahan discovered on his travels was "a great, possibly endless, confluence of worlds. They are all America, but they are all different." (298-99). During his time in Fort Lee, New Jersey, Callahan flipped between two almost identical versions of the town. One was the Fort Lee in our version of earth; the other was called Leabrook. In Fort Lee, Callahan stayed at the Sunrise Hotel and worked at the Fort Lee Homestyle Diner. In Leabrook, he stayed at the Sunset Motel and worked at the Leabrook Homestyle Diner. These parallel towns had slightly different histories. When Callahan was paid in Fort Lee, Grant was on the fifties, Jackson was on the twenties, and Hamilton was on the singles. But in Leabrook, Lincoln was on the fifties and someone named Chadbourne was on the tens. In the Leabrook reality, Spiro Agnew was president and NASA hoped to begin a terraforming program in outer space.

In the later novels, we realize that Callahan is not the only person to know of parallel Americas located in parallel worlds. In fact, at least two of Roland's ka-mates come from alternate Americas. In the New York City where Eddie Dean was born, Co-Op City is located in Brooklyn, not the Bronx. In Susannah Dean's New York, the A train stops at Christopher Street Station, which it doesn't in our world. As Eddie Dean says to himself when he finally becomes aware of the vastness of the multiverse:

•••

Other worlds. Perhaps an infinite number of worlds, all of them spinning on the axle that was the Tower. All of them were similar, but there were differences. Different politicians on the currency. Different makes of automobiles—Takuro Spirits instead of Datsuns, for instance—and different major league baseball teams. In these worlds, one of which had been decimated by a plague called the superflu, you could time-hop back and forth, past and future. Because... Because in some vital way, they aren't the real world. Or if they're real, they're not the key world (*Song of Susannah*, 200).

• • •

In Stephen King's multiverse, there are thousands of parallel worlds and twin worlds. These parallel worlds can give us comfort, since we know (as does Susannah Dean), that we can find twins of our dead loved ones in these other realities, and so perhaps find happiness even in the face of grief. But these other worlds are not the true worlds. In the true worlds, time moves in one direction only, and what's done can't be undone. These true worlds are Keystone World, which is our world, and Tower Keystone, which is Roland's.

Keystone World and Tower Keystone are twins. They are the templates upon which all other realities are based. The linchpin of time/space exists in each, but the forms it takes are different. In our world, the nexus of the multiverse takes the form of a delicate rose, and in Mid-World, it takes the form of a Tower.

In terms of imagery, the Rose and Tower are seemingly opposed. The rose is traditionally feminine, the Tower, masculine. Yet it is in the joining of the male and the female that new life comes into being, and universes are born. At

Twins and Twinning in Stephen King's Dark Tower Novels

the beginning of the Dark Tower series, Roland's quest is a masculine ideal. He is a loner who shoots before thinking, a man who has abandoned his heart. But Roland's discovery of the existence of the rose coincides with his rediscovery of his heart and his ability to love. It is only when Roland realizes that the delicate rose must be protected every bit as much as the Tower must be simultaneously preserved, that Roland's healing, and his redemption, become possible.

VII: Conclusion

Central to the Dark Tower mythos is the fact that Roland's world and our world are twins, and that the universe is replete with doubles, twins, twinners, echoes, parallel dimensions and parallel worlds. In the Dark Tower books, the universe is a house of mirrors where characters disappear only to reappear again in slightly altered guises, and where not even death can destroy ka's constant cycle of reincarnation. This doubling is so profound that one could argue that the Dark Tower series serves not just as the Jupiter of King's literary solar system, as he has attested, but also as the subconscious of King's vast oeuvre. It is a repository of archetypal images that are fundamentally important both to the writer and to the architecture of his fiction.

For Stephen King, twinning is a necessary part of the creative process. As his character Thad Beaumont says in *The Dark Half*: "All the times I've talked about writing... Hundreds of lectures, thousands of classes, and I don't believe I ever said a single word about a fiction-writer's grasp of the twin realities that exist for him—one in the real world and one in the manuscript world" (186). For King, a writer always has at least two selves, "the one who exists in the normal world... and the one who creates worlds" (*The Dark Half*, 333).

In *The Dark Tower*, Roland and Eddie find a magical doorway near a lakeside house in Maine called Cara Laughs. Unlike most of the magical and mechanical doorways they find in the novels that lead to other *wheres* and *whens*, this magical door—located in the middle of a beautiful bright light filled with beings from other worlds—is a doorway to anywhere. As Roland says, "It's not a door of the old people but of the Prim... It'll take us to the place we want, if we concentrate hard enough" (132). This door is a scrap of the original magic left over from when the world was born. It also happens to be the house that Stephen King is destined to buy. The light from which the beings emanate is a manifestation of the mind's magic, a magic that is as powerful as the one that gave birth to the universe. We can suppose that every writer or artist has such a door, since it is the fount of light that we call creativity and creative inspiration.

For Stephen King, the human imagination is a great gift, and is also the ultimate doorway between worlds. Our psyches are haunted houses, filled with voices and visions. We are not one person but many people, and we carry with us not only our hidden selves but our alternate futures and ghostly secrets. The universe, too, is a haunted place, filled with dreams and possibilities. It is so vast that true death does not have a place there. Somewhere, in some alternate or parallel dimension, we, and our loved ones, live on. The wheel of ka turns, and we turn with it. Perhaps we wear other guises or other names, but life continues to be life, and death has no dominion.

•••

Bibliography for "Twins and Twinning in Stephen King's Dark Tower Novels" by Robin Furth

Clark, Brian, "The Twin Motif in Comparative Mythology." (nd) http://www.astrosynthesis.com.au.

Cozzens, Lisa. "The Civil Rights Movement 1955-1965." *African American History.* http://fledge.watson.org/~lisa/blackhistory/civilrights-55-65 (25 May 1998).

Hankoff, Leon D. "Why the Healing Gods are Twins." *Yale Journal of Biology and Medicine* 50(3), 1977:307-319 http://www.ncbi.nlm.nih.gov/pmc/articles/PMC2595421.

Kanes, Candace, "Pownal State School and the Issue of Institutionalization." www.mainememory.net.

King, Stephen, *The Dark Half* (London: Hodder & Stoughton, 1989).

King, Stephen, *The Dark Tower* (Hampton Falls, New Hampshire: Donald M. Grant in association with Scribner, 2004).

King, Stephen, *The Drawing of the Three* (New York: Plume-Penguin, 1989).

King, Stephen, *The Gunslinger* (New York: Plume-Penguin, 1988).

King, Stephen, *The Gunslinger: Revised edition* (New York: Plume-Penguin, 2003).

King, Stephen, "The Little Sisters of Eluria," *Everything's Eventual: 14 Dark Tales* (New York: Scribner, 2002).

King, Stephen, *Song of Susannah.* (Hampton Falls, New Hampshire: Donald M. Grant in association with Scribner, 2004).

King, Stephen, *The Waste Lands* (New York: Plume-Penguin, 1989).

King, Stephen, *The Wind Through the Keyhole* (Hampton Falls, New Hampshire: Donald M. Grant in association with Scribner, 2012).

King, Stephen, *Wizard and Glass* (New York: Plume-Penguin, 1997).

King, Stephen, *Wolves of the Calla* (Hampton Falls, New Hampshire: Donald M. Grant in association with Scribner, 2003).

Pearlman, Karen, "Jim Crow Era Recalled in Rail Car Project." San Diego Union-Tribune, 2015. http://www.utsandiego.com/news/2012/feb/08/jim-crow-era-recalled-in-rail-car-project/.

Vaidman, Lev, "Many-Worlds Interpretation of Quantum Mechanics", *The Stanford Encyclopedia of Philosophy* (Winter 2014 Edition), Edward N. Zalta (ed.), http://plato.stanford.edu/archives/win2014/entries/qm-manyworlds/.

King Since Scribner

KEVIN QUIGLEY

Throughout his vast career, Stephen King has occasionally written novels that function as statements of purpose. With 1986's *It*, he largely put paid to his long-running theme of children vs. monsters (though this would resurface later in *Desperation*). With *Misery* in 1987, King chose to show the world that he could write without supernatural concerns. In 1991's *Needful Things*, he blew up his oft-visited small town of Castle Rock as a way of subverting complacency. Responding to criticisms that he faltered at writing believable female characters, King crafted 1992's *Gerald's Game* and *Dolores Claiborne*.

His biggest artistic and commercial shift, though, came in 1998. For the first time since 1979, King changed publishers. Believing he was being taken for granted at Viking and New American Library, he moved to the prestigious Simon & Schuster, and their imprint, Scribner. *Bag of Bones*, his first Scribner novel, was billed as "A Haunted Love Story" and included blurbs from respected mainstream novelists Amy Tan and Gloria Naylor. The book cover was largely white—a remove from the dark and occasionally lurid

Viking covers—and King's name, while prominent, stood out in a thin, elegant serif font. The implication seemed obvious: though King had successfully written non-horror books with Viking (*Different Seasons* springs to mind), he was always *sold* as a horror novelist.

Through marketing and perception, it seemed, Stephen King was trying for a fresh start, and perhaps a new audience. One of King's favorite preoccupations has long been introducing themes and motifs in his work, then exploring them in subsequent books and stories from every conceivable angle until they are exhausted. While his earliest books— his first decade or so—focused largely on children in peril and the parents being unable (or unwilling) to save them, his later work shifted to more adult concerns: writers and writing, mortality, God, and the nature of free will. Starting with *Bag of Bones*, King would work to hone those earlier interests even further, while expanding on new, fresh themes that would become the backbone of his Scribner output.

Love and Sex

Love has always been a crucial element in King's fiction, but in much of his early fiction, it is twisted, tragic, or downright harmful. Family bonds are often dangerous: note the destructive mother-daughter relationship in *Carrie*, the tragically flawed parents at the centers of *Rage*, *The Shining*, and *Firestarter*, and the array of poisonous parents of *It*. Obsessive love—eclipsing friendship, family, and eventually reality— overshadows *Christine*, *The Gunslinger*, *Pet Sematary*, and *Roadwork*—these latter two exploring a parent's natural love of a child becoming the unnatural obsession with the *idea* of a child. Ostensibly good marriages fall apart, as in

Cujo, and promising love affairs are cut short by tragedy, like those in *'Salem's Lot* and *The Dead Zone*. King's first real look at a messy and complicated—but workable—version of love was in *The Tommyknockers*, opening the way for the similarly nuanced takes on adult love in *The Dark Half*, *Needful Things*, and *Insomnia*.

King's early fictional relationship with sex was also problematic. The couples in *Cujo*, "Rita Hayworth and Shawshank Redemption," and "Something to Tide You Over" are undone by extramarital affairs, sexual abuse rears its head in *It* (and to some degree in *Rage*), homosexuality is seen as either odd (*The Stand*, *The Long Walk*) or damaging (*It* again), and the perverted sexuality perpetrated by the ghosts in *The Shining* and the malicious female presence in *Christine* work to underscore King's seemingly singular view of sex as something bizarre to be frightened of. Most of King's 1990s work only perpetuated these thoughts, with marital rape in *Rose Madder*, incest in *Dolores Claiborne*, and both *Desperation* and *Gerald's Game* insisting that kinky sex is inherently harmful.

In *Bag of Bones*, we are, for almost the first time, presented with a long marriage that is both loving and sexually healthy. "We are often overcome on the couch," Mike Noonan remembers his wife, Johanna, saying, and it's a memory rife with poignancy. Mike's later lust for Mattie Devore is presented frankly, as a fact rather than something to be wary of, despite the differences in their ages.

There's a dose of poisoned sexuality and love on the outskirts of both of King's 1999 books, *The Girl Who Loved Tom Gordon* and *Hearts in Atlantis*. In the former, the fallout of her parents' disintegrated marriage in part precipitates

Trisha McFarland's harrowing journey through the woods; later, a subplot involving a suspected pedophile comes into play. In *Hearts*, Bobby Garfield's mother is chained to the (perhaps false) memories of her horrible marriage, and she eventually becomes the victim of a brutal sexual assault. However, through the character of Carole Gerber, King is able to continue his exploration of smart, believable relationships. While Carole is a complex, layered character, she also functions symbolically, working as a romantic ideal for both young Bobby Garfield and college-age Pete Riley. Pete's relationship with Carole also awakens him to a larger worldview and an understanding of his relationship to it; through her reason and will, he is able to keep himself out of Vietnam, perhaps saving his life.

It's worth noting that young romances of this sort in King's earlier novels—especially *'Salem's Lot, The Dead Zone, Christine,* and *Wizard & Glass*—invariably ended in tragedy. Not so here, pointing the way toward the gentle love stories at the heart of *11/22/63* and *Joyland*.

With *Lisey's Story* (2006), King takes a quantum leap toward exploring the ins and outs of a long romance. The push for King's "marriage novel" echoed that of *Bag of Bones*: Nicholas Sparks (author of *The Notebook*) and Michael Chabon (author of Pulitzer Prize-winner *The Amazing Adventures of Kavalier & Clay*) were quoted on the back cover in lieu of horror genre writers to tout the book's crossover appeal.

Inside, we are witness to the complicated relationship between Pulitzer Prize winner Scott Landon, and his wife, Lisey. Theirs is a good marriage, but with darkness burbling beneath it, mostly due to Scott's terrifying past. One interesting sequence involves Lisey's and Scott's extended stay in Germany, marred by Scott's writer's block and increased drinking. Both he and Lisey escape into frequent, nearly feral sex; Lisey later admits to herself that while the sex was satisfying and exciting, it left her uneasy. For readers following King's handling of sexuality since his earliest novels, culminating in the injurious depiction of bondage in *Gerald's Game*, it is fascinating to watch him unearthing complexities in sex he has never quite tackled before. Necessitated by his themes, King reveals that purely physical—even kinky—sex can exist (at least occasionally) inside a healthy, mutually satisfying marriage.

King refers to 2008's *Duma Key* as his "story of divorce," intending it as sort of a counterpoint to *Lisey's Story*. This is perhaps misleading. Divorce is certainly a dominant theme, but while it *impacts* the novel, it does not *define* it. Edgar Freemantle, a successful contractor, is severely injured on the job. His hip is crushed and he loses his right arm (another interpretation of divorce). More importantly, he loses his memory; it returns in fits and starts. The process, often verbally and sometimes physically violent, estranges his wife Pam and she leaves him. Then, Edgar starts to draw.

Interestingly, at crucial points, all of these "divorces" return—Edgar regains his memory, but also the use of his missing arm and his ex-wife, Pam. The persistence of things missing cements *Duma Key* as an even stronger spiritual cousin to *Bag of Bones* than *Lisey's Story*. In *The Girl Who Loved Tom Gordon*, Trisha McFarland's estranged parents use sex as solace when their little girl goes missing; here, Edgar and Pam reconnect sexually at a moment of both sorrow and triumph. There's a jovial frankness here, too, as when Edgar remembers that Pam sometimes laughs deeply when she has an orgasm.

We're treated to an unusually honest—and slightly awkward—conversation between Edgar and his daughter Ilse about extramarital affairs, and how it's possible to sometimes forgive them and sometimes not. King allows Edgar to have an opinion without moralizing or dismissing, a somewhat new take on the subject. There are hints of this sort of moral gray zone in *Cujo*, but most of that novel's deep tragedies spring directly from Donna's affair with Steve Kemp. In *The Mist*, David Drayton and Amanda Jeffries—both married—have solace sex that is treated as a fact, without real exploration; even this is deeper than Dick Bowden recalling that he is "sometimes unfaithful with his secretary" in "Apt Pupil," and that it has no bearing on his "*family* life." In *The Dead Zone*, Johnny and the married Sarah make love that is beneficial to both of them, but it springs out of sadness. Sarah says, "'I think it's wrong, but I can't help it. It's wrong but it's right. It's *fair*.'" While this sequence resonates, it's treated as symbolic by both King and the characters: "'Once will have put paid to everything,'" Sarah says, and when it's over, "'Time's up.'"

By contrast, Edgar assures his daughter Ilse that his one-night stand with his ex-wife was strictly comfort, though in the narrative, Edgar tells us a different story. "It was *not* strictly comfort, but what it had been was something I wasn't prepared to explore with my daughter. Or myself, for that matter." King's willingness to allow Edgar conflict speaks to the complexities of Edgar and Pam's marriage and divorce; theirs is a nuanced, realistic relationship we've rarely seen in King's work.

After all this progressive momentum, the destructive marriages and gruesome rapes found between the covers of *Full Dark, No Stars* might seem like a setback. On the contrary, these novellas function as *Desperation* did with King's seemingly retired motif of a child with special powers fighting monsters: the time away has given King time to refine and enhance these themes. "Big Driver," the most straightforward of the *Full Dark* novellas, finds King continuing a thread of fiction he first explored in the early 1990s with *Gerald's Game, Dolores Claiborne,* and *Rose Madder* (as well as, to some degree, *The Girl Who Loved Tom Gordon*), books about inherent female power, and how it is channeled to break out of bad situations. After Tess (no last name given) is raped and left for dead, "Big Driver" treats her mission of retribution not as a revenge fantasy or a single-minded rampage, but as a realistic depiction of a woman who has a necessary job to do. In a way, she reminds readers of *The Stand*'s Dayna Jurgins—similarly refusing to collapse into victimization—though Tess's heroism is more personal and singular. Throughout "Big Driver," Tess's complex personality—intelligent, serious, funny, frightened, determined—shines through; she is instantly relatable and constantly interesting. Late in the story, when she believes she has killed the wrong man, she considers suicide, proof that Tess has not become some sort of killing machine. King allows for no easy answers in this or any of the other stories in *Full Dark, No Stars,* simply people making overwhelming decisions and finding out whether they can live with the consequences.

We find King once again working with the motif of marriage in the bookend novellas, "1922" and "A Good Marriage," the latter of whose title is both true and ironic. Unlike the bad husbands in King's female empowerment novels of the 1990s, "Good Marriage"'s innocuously named Bob Anderson is as good to his wife, Darcy, as she is to him. Darcy's discovery that Bob is a serial killer changes the paradigm of their marriage completely. King hinted at the notion of a husband's hidden darkness running parallel to his otherwise perfect marriage in *Lisey's Story*. Here, King both expands upon and hones the concept—the "bad-gunky" Scott Landon must release in *Lisey's* is similar to Bob Anderson's compulsion to murder. The crucial difference is that Scott Landon managed to channel his darker impulses into the act of creation, where Bob Anderson can only destroy. The final death of "A Good Marriage" also recalls that of *Lisey's Story*, though here it feels more immediate and personal, and thus more impactful.

If "A Good Marriage" interprets and refines the themes in *Lisey's Story*, "1922" expands those of *Dolores Claiborne*. The surface similarities are as obvious as the method of murder; in both, a bad spouse ends up dead at the bottom of a well. But where *Dolores Claiborne* is essentially a mainstream story with moments of horror centered around Joe St. George's death, here, the story begins dark and grows darker, heightening the more grisly aspects of Wilford James' murder of his wife, Arlette. The distinction here is intent: where Dolores Claiborne's motives were driven by compassion, Wilford James' are driven by greed. At its most basic, "1922" shows what might have happened if Joe St. George had murdered Dolores instead of the other way around.

After the "harsh" tales of *Full Dark, No Stars*, we find King picking up where *Bag of Bones* left off in *11/22/63*. It's a big book with big ideas, a science fiction construct on the outside allowing King to tell a compelling historical novel on the inside. At the center, though, is the book's heart: a sweet, unhurried romance that proves to be one of Stephen King's most believable and compelling. King has obviously grown since *The Tommyknockers*' and *Rose Madder*'s take on adult love stories, but what's most exciting is his growth since signing with Scribner. In *Bag of Bones*, Mike Noonan and Mattie Devore are both detail-rich characters with their own backstories and reasons for falling in love, but by the novel's necessity, the affair is a little uneven. Their differences in age, power, and—interestingly—finances are roadblocks, not to mention the shadows of their dead spouses. While it's a far more realistic take on love, however, Mattie's death takes on the same symbolic weight as Susan Norton's in *'Salem's Lot*, or Susan Delgado's in *Wizard & Glass*, making their love story a tragedy.

11/22/63 deliberately averts this sort of tragedy, even though the love of Jake Epping's life, Sadie Dunhill, dies, sort of. King devotes a lot of pages to developing their love affair—it's slow, sweet, and crackling. Managing to respect and acknowledge the mores of the early 1960s, King allows Sadie and Jake an explicitly sexual relationship, as well. The return of Sadie's ex-husband, not to mention her subsequent disfigurement, can be seen as a sort of symbolic "punishment" for their affair, but the book doesn't treat it as such. What we are left with is something unique in King's canon—an unhurried, convincing adult romance that flirts with disaster but doesn't succumb to it.

If *11/22/63* picks up the emotional threads from *Bag of Bones*, then *Joyland*, King's second Hard Case Crime novel, resumes the nostalgic feel of the young-adult romance of "Hearts In Atlantis." The year is 1973, seven years removed from "Hearts," and Devin Jones, our college-age protagonist, is just starting to realize that his first long-term relationship is coming to an end. Without the tumult of Vietnam to serve as the backdrop, King allows us—and Dev—time to work through the breakup itself, while spending the summer in the employ of the Joyland amusement park. King hasn't much explored the love lives of young adults before, but when he has, it almost always ends in tragedy. Death comes to young lovers in *Christine*, *'Salem's Lot,* and *Wizard and Glass,* and a coma separates Johnny and Sarah in *The Dead Zone*. Here, King does justice to Dev by treating "just a breakup" as seriously as he treated the aftermath of Jo Noonan's death in *Bag of Bones*. The details sell it: Wendy, Dev's ex, just sort of stumbles away from him, and it devastates him. Dev listens to sad music, stops eating, and has vague "suicidal iterations," which even he knows aren't that serious. At one point, Dev recognizes that his breakup isn't all that important in the scheme of things, but also that it *is*, and that, to his lingering dismay, he will likely never completely get over her.

Layered on the story of Dev's breakup are the twin stories of friendship and sexual awakening. Dev thinks of his Joyland summer as the last summer of his childhood. Autumn, then, is his first as an adult. He says goodbye to a friend who might have been more, and there's a passionate goodbye kiss that serves as a faint echo of Bill Denbrough and Beverly Rogan making love in *It*. As Bill sent Bev on her way to a life with Ben Hanscom, so does Dev send Erin Cook onto her future with Tom Kennedy. It's closure for everyone involved; later, when Erin visits Dev back at Joyland, her kisses are strictly sisterly.

Then there's Annie Ross, a decade older than Dev and at first as adversarial with Dev as Roland had been with Susan in *Wizard and Glass*. Later, Annie becomes his first lover. Sarah's admonition from *The Dead Zone* creeps back: Annie tells him, "It can only be this once. You have to understand that." King, however, subverts the collocation by allowing Dev and Annie *three* times together—enough time to get it right. "The first time was embarrassing," he recalls. "The second time was good. The third...man, the third time was the charm."

It's also the last time, and what's important here in the context of King's fiction is that it doesn't directly lead to grief and pain. Both immediately after and in the long-term, Dev and Annie remain friends, albeit platonically. While there's some precedent here—*The Tommyknockers*, *Duma Key*, in a way—this is one of the first times a King character has lost his virginity in a way that doesn't lead to grief and sadness. Even in "Hearts in Atlantis," though neither Pete nor Carole die after their first time, Carole leaves college the next afternoon and Pete never sees her again. In *Joyland*, the sex doesn't seem *symbolic*, even if it is Dev's first time. It just seems like sex—good, exciting sex that neither one regrets.

Part of *Joyland*'s success is in its evocation of the early 1970s, which ties it not only with "Hearts in Atlantis" (in many ways, *Joyland* reads like a spiritual sequel to that novella), but also with King's oldest novels. There's a certain flavor to Stephen King's 1970s books that goes deeper than theme and tone and even feel, especially in the smaller, more personal stories like *The Shining* and *'Salem's Lot* and *The Dead Zone*. The books are certainly "of their time," but it's more than that: it's a distinct spirit that's difficult to pin down and even harder to describe.

Nostalgia

Those impetuses and ideas clarified in *Joyland* are not new to King's work, especially during his Scribner years. Memories, lost projects, and loose ends have found new life in King's career since 1998, with King not only rediscovering forgotten stories and discarded concepts, but finding vital value in them. His renewed interest in some of his oldest ideas and work has allowed contemporary readers more access to King's undiscovered past than ever before.

Joyland began life in King's early career as a novel called *Darkshine*, about a psychic boy trapped in an amusement park. He took those basic components and transformed them into *The Shining*, removing the amusement park milieu in favor of a more remote setting. While King would return to the concept of a haunted amusement park occasionally in his career—notably in the short story "Riding the Bullet" and the fragment "Skybar"—it is with *Joyland* that King truly returns to the bones of his initial concept. Stunningly, he also somehow regains the *flavor* of the fiction written concurrently. King's 1970s novels come from such a distinct time, place, and mindset in King's career that, by their nature, the stories reflect who and where their author was when they were written. While *Joyland* feels fresh and reads fast it also seems like a lost book from King's first days as a struggling writer with something to prove.

Achieving such a unique tonal re-immersion is a singular success, but it isn't without precedent.

Readers need only look to 2007's *Blaze*, which, until its publication, was something of a legend in Stephen King circles. King first discussed the book a quarter-century before

King Since Scribner

its eventual release, in his afterword to *Different Seasons*. Following the publication of *Carrie*, King presented his editor with two new manuscripts—*Second Coming* (which would eventually become *'Salem's Lot*) and *Blaze*, the story of a mentally challenged giant who decides to kidnap a child for ransom money. The first was a new kind of vampire novel, the second an *Of Mice and Men* pastiche. King's editor determined that the vampire book was the better of the two, lamenting that King was going to get "typed" as a horror writer. King didn't seem to mind much, *'Salem's Lot* was published, and *Blaze* got stuck in a trunk.

Interest in *Blaze* didn't stop there. As a cottage industry of books *about* Stephen King cropped up, interest grew in every shadowy avenue of the man's writing, including his unpublished work. Michael Collings' *The Many Facets of Stephen King* and George Beahm's seminal *Stephen King Companion* discussed *Blaze* in greater detail than King had; much later, Spignesi's *Lost Work of Stephen King* devoted a whole chapter to *Blaze*. Like the two other unpublished pre-*Carrie* King novels, *The Aftermath* and *Sword in the Darkness*, *Blaze*, it seemed, was going to be relegated to mythic, unread status forever.

This held true until 2006, when King suddenly and surprisingly let it slip that *Blaze*, after thirty-five years, was going to be published. Further, he was considering it another "lost" Bachman book, in the same vein as *The Regulators*... the major difference was that, unlike *The Regulators*, *Blaze* really *was* a lost book. King explains the decision in the "Full Disclosure" foreword, "The Bachman name is on it because it's the last novel from 1966-1973, which was that gentleman's period of greatest productivity."

Editing from his very early draft, King re-wrote *Blaze* in the noir style, utilizing "dry, flat tones" and leaving the time frame intentionally vague. King also reveals that he'd written using the tools of old noir writers, employing a typeface font and editing in pencil; these glimpses into King's writing process always illuminate the stories from which they spring. All these elements taken into consideration, *Blaze* would have the feel of the early Bachman novels, a similar style, a familiar structure—an indicator of what King would later achieve with *Joyland*.

King's renewed interest in *Blaze* may have been stirred by the unexpected attention to one of his *other* unpublished pre-*Carrie* novels, the aforementioned *Sword in the Darkness*. While King will likely never publish *Sword* in its entirety, in 2005, he allowed a significant portion of it to see the light. *Stephen King: Uncollected, Unpublished*, by King monographer Rocky Wood, featured Chapter 71 of the novel. Mostly a long, uninterrupted monologue by the character Edie Rowsmith, this chapter allows for a glimpse into the book-length work King was doing around the time *Rage* and *The Long Walk* were being constructed. It's a fascinating snapshot of King's development as a novelist.

While the complete manuscript of *Sword in the Darkness* (not to mention *The Aftermath*) will likely never be published for a mass audience, other early aborted novels and novel concepts *have* eventually made their way to the bestseller lists. When *11/22/63* was released in 2011, King released a promotional video explaining that he'd originally begun a version of the book in 1973—the year before *Carrie* was published. Back then, the novel was called *Split Track*, and King only got through fourteen pages before he put the book on a nearly forty-year hiatus.

There was significantly more to the early attempts at *Under the Dome*. In 1978, the year the original version of *The Stand* came out, King wrote about seventy pages of *Under the Dome* before putting it aside and, eventually, losing the manuscript. He took his second swing at the novel, now retitled *The Cannibals*, in 1981, and got a lot further—about 450 pages—before "hitting a wall." Later, King would believe this manuscript was also lost...until it turned up, mostly complete, in 2009. King seemed delighted by the discovery: "I'm amused by the antique quality of the typescript; this may have been the last thing I did on my old IBM Selectric before moving on to a computer system."

An interesting comment in light of what King chose to do next: in an unprecedented move, King decided to make *The Cannibals*—the first sixty pages, at least—available to his fans free of charge on his website via downloadable PDFs. As a bonus, readers would not simply be receiving the *story*, but would also be receiving copies of King's actual *pages*. Editing marks, word changes, even chapter title alterations abound, all scribbled in King's own hand over a typewritten manuscript. It was an extraordinary chance for readers to see a Stephen King story in progress. Not only would fans be able to compare King's "second effort" to write *Under the Dome* with the 1,074-page novel hitting bookstores mere months later, but they would be able to "watch" the story grow and change as it was happening.

Initially, King only released the first sixty pages of the manuscript for download; when *The Cannibals* proved popular and fans began clamoring for more, King published another sixty-two pages on his site. While these 122 pages are but a fraction of what King wrote before stopping, it's a bit of a miracle that *The Cannibals* was made available at all. In his book, *The Lost Work of Stephen King* (1998), Stephen Spignesi offered no hope for King completists attempting to hunt down the aborted novel. "Chances of finding a copy? Zero." Now, it was available to anyone, anywhere, free of charge. The power of the Internet, at your service.

Speaking of the Internet, let's not forget King's 2000 experiment, *The Plant*. Between the years of 1982 and 1985, Stephen King published a serialized novel titled *The Plant* through his personal publishing house, Philtrum Press. The three installments were printed as chapbooks and distributed to those on King's Christmas list (skipping an installment in 1984 and instead sending out the Philtrum Press version of *The Eyes of the Dragon*). King ceased publication of the story with the third segment, feeling that the story was uncomfortably similar to that of the film *Little Shop of Horrors*. Collectors went crazy for the original installments, with each segment commanding outlandish prices on the secondary market. Many clamored for a continuation of the story, but it soon became obvious that King had abandoned the project permanently.

Or so it seemed.

In 2000, King announced plans to return to the *The Plant*—not only to the story, but to the method of delivery. Combining the publishing models of his wildly successful *Green Mile* and "Riding the Bullet" gambits, Stephen King was going to publish his epistolary story serially—one section a month, for a fee—and he was going to do it online. In the more experimental days before ebooks were the norm, the idea was a risky one. Some minor controversy erupted almost at once, mostly among those who didn't think King should be charging for an ebook at all. Still, the initial reaction to *The Plant* was a roaring success. For King fanatics who had heard of *The Plant* but never read it, this was a chance to finally get their eyes on a long-lost King work; for casual fans, here was something brand-new. Starting with Part 4, *everyone* got something new, including those who had paid exorbitant fees for the first three chapbooks on the secondary market. While King halted the novel after Part 6—King later stated, "the story never picked me up and carried me"—*The Plant* remains a project unique in King's career: an unfinished, unpublished novel that was finally released to the public and got a second chance at life.

King's novels aren't the only fictional revenants making recent appearances. Though King had stated in the foreword to *Nightmares & Dreamscapes* that he would no longer be publishing "old" stories in his new collections, King's 1977 short story, "The Cat From Hell" appears in his 2008 collection, *Just After Sunset* (in the afterword, King explains that he simply thought the story had already been collected). King's 1982 graphic fiction collection *Creepshow* contained two adaptations of previously-published prose stories, "The Crate" (1979, in *Gallery* magazine) and "Weeds" (*Cavalier*, 1976, and adapted as "The Lonesome Death of Jordy Verrill"). Four decades later, both stories would appear in separate volumes of the Cemetery Dance anthology series, *Shivers*. The impossibly rare, vintage, uncollected, previously *unpublished* story from 1971/72 titled "The Old Dude's Ticker"—an Edgar Allen Poe pastiche—finally surfaced in 2000, in *The Big Book of NECON*, a collection of work selected from twenty years of the Northeast Regional Fantasy and Horror Convention program books. Reaching even further back, we find King's first professional fiction sale, "The Glass Floor," which appeared in the sixth issue of Robert A.W. Lowndes' pulp magazine, *Startling Mystery Stories*, in 1967. The story got a brief airing in 1990 for *Weird Tales* magazine, then went back into hiding until 2013, when it was published in issue #68 of *Cemetery Dance* magazine.

Perhaps, though, none of these hold a candle to the 2013 publication of the poem, *The Dark Man*. First published in 1969, this poem is one of the most important of King's career. Between 1969 and 1971, King published seven poems, on par with his short story output at the time...then stopped. Almost none of those early poems have been included in King's official collections, which is especially mystifying, since work like "The Hardcase Speaks" and "The Dark Man" poems are direct thematic antecedents to later prose. "The Dark Man" poem in particular is vital, as it serves as an introduction to one of King's most enduring villains: Randall Flagg. Publisher Cemetery Dance opted to publish this short work as a stand-alone book, festooned with art by frequent King collaborator Glenn Chadbourne, making *The Dark Man* the Stephen King book with the earliest date on the copyright page.

These journeys into the past shed light on the sometimes hard-to-find work King has done previously—or parallel—to his more famous career as a bestselling author. But what of the bestsellers themselves? Following his move to Scribner, King began exploring the stories that came *after* the stories he'd written for previous publishers. In 2000, King and Straub returned to Jack Sawyer, the child adventurer at the heart of 1984's *The Talisman* (published by Viking) with the sequel *Black House*. This novel is a complex, challenging read, and—at Straub's suggestion—includes plot elements connecting it intricately with King's Dark Tower series, making the book perhaps the least casually approachable book in Stephen King's canon. Still, fans of the *Dark Tower* novels had reason for celebration; aside from some elements of 1999's *Hearts in Atlantis*, this was the first peek into the saga of Roland Deschain since *Wizard and Glass* (published by Grant in 1997). Tower fans would have to wait until 2003 for another full *Dark Tower* book, *Wolves of the Calla*, after which the final two books—*Song of Susannah* and *The Dark Tower*—followed in rapid succession.

As we've seen, though, in King's career, *final* doesn't always mean *for-real final*. In early December of 2009, King announced his intention to write one of two new books: an interstitial novel of the Dark Tower series called *The Wind Through the Keyhole*...and *Doctor Sleep*, a sequel to his 1977 Doubleday novel, *The Shining*. (It is interesting that the three sequels—or series of sequels—King has written since joining Scribner are connected to books from three different publishers). King ended up writing both books, with *Doctor Sleep* following *Joyland* and *The Dark Man*—both different sorts of journeys into the past—in 2013.

The Wind Through the Keyhole is a somewhat different animal. Published in 2012, the book serves as a bridging story between *Wizard & Glass* and *Wolves of the Calla*. As with *Joyland*, King manages here to capture a specific tonal feel, in this case that of the first four books in the Dark Tower series. (While there are plenty of merits to the final three books of the series, they achieved a different, often less whimsical feel of the preceding books, especially that of *The Drawing of the Three* and *The Waste Lands*). Not only did *Keyhole* revive a series thought to be completed, but it's also a deeper look into the fictional past of the series itself. This is an important distinction, as no book could logically follow the seventh book in the series without significantly altering the structure of the story. By placing *The Wind Through the Keyhole* in the middle of the Dark Tower series, King allows the overarching theme of repetition to continue, and it's this theme more than any other that has captured King's fascination since 1998.

We begin with a little story called "That Feeling, You Can Only Say What It Is In French."

• • •

Hell is Repetition
From small things, big things someday come.
Mere months before Stephen King released *Bag of Bones* with Scribner, *The New Yorker* quietly published his odd little story with that odd, long name: "That Feeling, You Can Only Say What It Is In French." *Déjà vu*, in shorter words, and in King's short afterword to the story, he explains his message:

• • •

I think this story is about Hell. A version of it where you are condemned to do the same thing over and over again. Existentialism, baby, what a concept; paging Albert Camus. There's an idea that Hell is other people. My idea is that it might be repetition.

• • •

Perhaps ironically, this isn't King's first time at this particular rodeo. The 1995 story, "Luckey Quarter," played with the concept, and any of King's tales of ghosts and creatures with a cyclical existence (*It*, for example, or even Randall Flagg) touch on the theme, but "That Feeling" is where King clarifies it as a central concern. In 1998's *Storm of the Century*, King further cements the concept, as nearly eternal Andre Linoge reveals realtor Robbie Beals' deepest secret: "You were with a whore in Boston when your mother died in Machias... She choked to death calling your name," he claims. Then he ominously promises, "She's waiting for you in hell. And she's turned cannibal. When you get there she's going to eat you alive. Over and over and over again. Because that's what hell's all about—repetition." Later, in the guise of Beals' mother, Linoge gets more specific: "I'll be waiting for you in hell, Robbie, and when you get there, I'll have a spoon. I'm going to use it on your eyes. I'm going to eat your eyes, Robbie, over and over again, because hell is repetition. Born in sin, come on in."

Since, King has explored this idea from several angles, often on small canvases. In 2008's "N.," King's story concerning the horrifying notion of communicable insanity, a psychiatrist's patient falls into an obsessive-compulsive disorder so severe that he ends up killing himself. The psychiatrist is then compelled to repeat the same actions, and the cycle of compulsion and suicide spreads. With "Herman Wouk is Still Alive," the character of Brenda brings to mind the similarly desperate (and similarly "lucky") Darlene Pullen of "Luckey Quarter," though—initially—without Darlene's dual senses of self-awareness and doom. Brenda's increasing desperation over her suffocating life comes to a head when she finally considers the future, and how her choices will have repercussions for generations. Here, Brenda's growing awareness of the concept of generational repetition provides the story's violent denouement.

One of the more pervasive uses of this theme is in King's *11/22/63*, in which a doorway to the past—specifically 1958—allows Jake Epping to change the world of the present. There are rules to this particular form of time travel: the person who goes back to the past always arrives at the same time and place, and each trip back to 1958 resets every change he'd made on a previous trip, wiping the slate clean. Jake's first few trips to 1958 underline the dilemma: if he's made any mistakes in the past, he can correct them with another trip, but *every* change he's made has been erased, even the "good" ones. This setup provides the basis for the unsettling repercussions at the book's finale, and Epping's decision not to repeat his life in the past is a twist on King's central theme: Epping has the *choice* to repeat his life over. In his 2013 short story, "Afterlife," King applies these ideas to purgatory: William Andrews, who has his own stockpile of misdeeds buried in his past, is given a choice about how to react to the bad things he's done in his life, and to the people he's hurt. The choice to live his life over is his, but Andrews doesn't retain the knowledge of this being a reset life. This opens King up to ask some of the big questions of his career: whether free will is real, whether sin is ingrained, and whether people really have the ability to change their natures.

Of course, King finds his most fertile ground for these questions in his *magnum opus*, the Dark Tower series. In the prequel story, "The Little Sisters of Eluria," King states, "Ka was a wheel; it was also a net from which one never escaped." Ka—or fate, or destiny—offered hints of repetition in the earlier books in the series, notably in the similarity between gunslinger Roland Deschain's current compatriots and those he had as a child (especially in *Wizard & Glass*).

King Since Scribner

In his re-write of the first book of the series, *The Gunslinger*, King provided a hint to the nature of the series in the new subtitle, "Resumption"...a subtitle repeated in *The Dark Tower*, the final book in the series.

It is with this concluding volume that King really hits his theme home. After seven books and twenty-two years, Roland of Gilead finally enters the Dark Tower. His climb to the top is flanked by rooms looking in on moments from Roland's long past; at the top is a door simply reading ROLAND. Now, King's intentions come clear: the adage *ka, like a wheel*, the subtitle RESUMPTION, his efforts to connect this final Dark Tower book to his first. Roland steps through the door only to realize that he has reached this goal time and time again, forgetting his journey to the Tower each time. The last sentence of this book is the first sentence of *The Gunslinger*: "The man in black fled across the desert, and the gunslinger followed."

The effectiveness of this finale is dependent upon the reader. King seems to be indicating here that the journey is far more important than the destination, but he also may be signifying that Roland is living out his personal version of Hell (though not without possible redemption; there are indications that this next journey may be his last. There's also the real world to consider: *The Dark Tower* ended up not being the final book in the series.). By initially concluding the series in this manner, King is both able to underscore the importance of quest above conclusion and avoid the disappointment of a possibly unfulfilling conventional ending. However, readers may view this sort of ending as a prevarication, not caring about what King views as his larger concerns to his fiction or to the series. That King, in-story, concedes that this is a controversial choice for an ending—that it, indeed, is not an ending at all—is fascinating and he seems angry for having to write it. The tone in his disclaimer is almost bitter. "Endings are heartless," he states. "Ending is just another word for goodbye."

Perhaps, then, he is subverting his own message. In decades past, King jumped publishers because they weren't treating him or his work seriously enough, and was rewarded with a career that defied all expectations. Reacting similarly to a feeling of complacency at his then-current publisher, King jumped ship again in 1998, ushering in a new era and a new audience. He's returned to towns he made famous in the past—Derry, specifically—and written new stories about old characters. A career in fiction, especially one as varied and as celebrated as King's, has peaks and valleys, but good ideas—like *The Dark Man,* like "The Glass Floor," like *The Plant*—have a way of coming around again, all the way from the beginning. If ka is a wheel, then yes, maybe repetition *can be* hell, like so many of his characters (and perhaps King himself) believe. But maybe, just sometimes, the opposite is true. If King's final statement in *The Dark Tower* means anything—if endings really are heartless, and "goodbye" is to be avoided—King seems to be arguing that sometimes, repetition is heaven.

Being a Non-US Stephen King Fan

HANS-ÅKE LILJA

Have you ever considered what it means to be a fan of someone that lives in a different country than you do? Well, often it's not really a problem because it's very rare that you need to meet the person and if it's someone in the music business the chances are pretty good that he or she will tour your country at least once in a while. But have you thought about what it means if you're a fan of an author? Well, I am and I have.

I'm in the exact situation of being a big fan of Stephen King's work and him being an American and I a Swede living in Sweden…you know that little country way up in the north. I've been a fan of King's work since I was in my early teens and that is coming up on 30 years now. Today I have found ways to make it easier for me, but back in the mid-80s, it was very different.

To be fair, I guess today's technology with the Internet and email and such have made it easier but still. In the 80s and 90s, if you lived in Sweden you probably didn't know that a new book was on the way until it actually appeared in the stores, and I worked in a bookstore. And by book I mean the US edition because you didn't really want to wait for the

Swedish edition which was always a year or two away. At the beginning of my King reading days I did read the books in Swedish but that was when there were a lot of books already translated and new ones coming once a year or so. Then, when I had read all the books that were translated, the problem started. I wanted more, and to get more I had no choice but to read the US or UK editions. And believe me, if English isn't your first language that can be a very daunting task. And, you never know in advance when a book was coming, and that was very frustrating.

Then, in the mid-90s, the Internet came and there you could find info about upcoming books. This, however, was when the average webpage was 95% text and 4% revolving skulls and maybe 1% book covers and other photos or pictures. So, even though the info was better, it was still hard to find and if you did find it you really didn't know what to do with it because the bookstores here in Sweden weren't really dying to order expensive hardbacks from the US or the UK, even if the books were written by Stephen King.

This was around the time when I started *Lilja's Library* (1996) mainly because there weren't many sites online that gave me the info I wanted about Stephen King and his books. There were some, and there were a lot of communities where King and his work were discussed, but what I felt the Internet needed was a one place where all this info was collected and that was what I was trying to do with *Lilja's Library*. And I think I have succeeded pretty well, if I may say so myself. Oh well, back to me sitting in Sweden in the mid-90s, wanting to know more about upcoming Stephen King books.

As the Internet bloomed, it got easier and easier to find out when new books were being released (today we know

Being a Non-US Stephen King Fan

about books almost a year in advance) and it was also getting easier and easier to buy the books online. But then it was time for the next hurdle...the cost of buying the books. As most of you know many of King's books are thick, very thick, and if a book is thick it's also very heavy, and if a book is heavy it's also very expensive to ship to Sweden. And this was the case with every King book released. No matter if you ordered it yourself or if you had a bookstore order it for you, the cost was often huge. Maybe a bit higher if a bookstore ordered it for you since they wanted to make a buck out of it as well. The upside with having a bookstore order it for you was that you didn't have to use your credit card online since that wasn't always a good thing to do back when the Internet was young. That aspect of it has improved but the cost is still a pain today, even if it has gotten a bit better over the years. If you order books from outside Sweden it's often very expensive to send them, in some cases as much as the book itself. And as if that wasn't enough, Swedish Customs charges you a fee to let you import the book to Sweden and then a fee because you imported the book and made them take out the first fee. Insane! So, a book that might cost around $35.00 in a book store in the US can cost around $80.00 or $90.00 to get here, in the worst case scenario. If you're lucky, and the customs miss that it's a bought book in the package, you can get away with $60.00 or $70.00.

Today the price of imported books in bookstores and online retailers has also gone down a bit because of the competition, and it's not as expensive as it was once. But if you want to read King's books as they are released, that's what you'll have to put up with. And even if you do, it might take you anywhere between one to four weeks for the book to arrive, and for most King fans, that is torture. The alternative is to wait between anything from one to sixteen (*The Dark Tower III: The Waste Lands*) years for a translated edition. Some books might never get translated (*The Colorado Kid*). And if you wait for the translated edition there is no guarantee that you'll get a good book. Well, King's story is still as good but the translation might not be.

Other things that affect you if you don't live in the US are things like stories published in magazines. Today many of those are also published on the magazines' websites so that you can access them there, but if not—and this was the case for a very long time—you will have a very hard time finding a copy of that magazine in Sweden. Maybe you would get lucky and your library would have the magazine, and you'd only had to wait about a month or so for their copy to arrive. Or maybe you know someone in the US who could get you a copy and send it to you, but most of the times it wasn't even worth the effort to try and find one.

And if you wanted to get a Limited Edition of one of King's books, forget it. Not only was it almost impossible to find out that they were done in time before they sold out (nowadays that's not a problem), but if you did they cost a lot (much more than the trade edition). With postage and insurance and custom fees and fees on custom fees you had to be pretty well set to be able to afford them. I remember when I bought a copy of *Six Stories*. It was when I had started *Lilja's Library* and had made some friends in the US who kept me updated on what was going on. I decided to get a copy and since it wasn't all that big and heavy I got it at a pretty fair price. Something I'm very happy about today.

Being a Non-US Stephen King Fan

Another thing that I love is audiobooks. I love listening to King's stories, preferably narrated by King himself, but here in Sweden fewer than ten books have been released as audiobooks. That is if you don't count the specialty audiobooks for the visually-impaired that you can get from the library. The only problem with those books is that they are so poorly done that you can't stand listening to them. The people producing them seem to reason that if you don't see well, you don't need to have any passion in a book. The people narrating them have voices that are on the same level all through the book, and it sounds like they are reading a grocery list. I know that people keep saying that King could sell his grocery list, but not like this. They are terrible and I feel so sorry for all of those that have to rely on those books to be able to hear King's fantastic stories. You could get the US or UK editions here as well but then again, they are hard to find in stores and you would have to order them yourself and the price will then have the shipping cost and the custom fee added.

So, what to do? Well, you could do what many fans in Sweden are doing and wait for the translated book. Or you could do what I did, start a website, build connections and make sure you know everything there is to know. Find people that can help you get what you want and pay for it. Or you could do something in-between. It's really up to each and every one of you out there who are King fans and don't live in the US or in the UK or even Germany where they are fairly quick with the translated editions. The UK editions are released close to the same day as the US, and the German editions come about a week later. With the Internet it's a lot easier to keep track of King and what he's about to publish so you should be able to find out what's coming and when. Then, it's up to you to decide when you want it, in what language and at what price.

Also, it might seem like I'm complaining about the cost of books, and let me make it clear that it's not the cost of the book itself that I'm complaining about but the extra cost that's added because the book has to be sent from the US to Sweden. And to all of you that work in the postal service all over the world, I do understand that you need to get paid for your services so it's really not *that* unfair that it costs so much, but it is very frustrating. And for King fans like me, the wait for getting a book is, as I said, pure torture.

One thing that has made it easier for all of us non-US fans is downloadable audiobooks and ebooks. Those you can order and you won't have to pay shipping costs or custom fees. Even better, you can start reading the book minutes after you've placed your order. So, even though I'm very much aware that a lot of fans don't see ebooks as "real" books, it has made life easier for us non-US King fans. That's a fact!

THE ROLE OF GOD IN STEPHEN KING'S *DESPERATION*

BILLY CHIZMAR

This essay is designed to examine the role of God in Stephen King's *Desperation* by investigating the question: "How does the Christian God of *Desperation* exhibit both love and cruelty, and which of these characteristics is more potent in God?" This essay focuses on this single novel while briefly mentioning several other of King's works, all of them with a single unifying feature, the subject of religion. In *Desperation*, there exists a God who is frequently involved and often intervenes in the affairs of the main characters. God's actions, both miracles and atrocities, are examined in this essay in an attempt to answer the research question. However, it becomes apparent that the line between God's love and God's cruelty is not as clear as one would anticipate, and there even exists a struggle to determine whether some of His interventions are inspired by mercy or manipulation.

An investigation into the various acts of God, as well as an analysis of characters' various reactions reveal that the holy miracles are not wholly good. Each involves some sinister twist, which assists God in achieving His goal of destroying the demon Tak, no matter the cost. King allows the reader to question the morality of sacrificing a few for the greater good, and offers ample opportunity for further exploration.

Because of this investigation, one is able to conclude that religion is capable of driving people to do unprecedented things, both good and evil. Furthermore, it is an individualized experience and it affects each person or character differently.

Introduction

A 1912 editorial from *The Biblical World* questions the existence of a higher power that would allow the pain, the destruction, and the rage present in the modern era. Many point to the multitude of crusades undertaken in God's name that resulted in utter destruction, or the harm religious fervor can cause even today. Modern radical groups driven by religious fanaticism are just one more reason for the contemporary human to be afraid of the capabilities of organized faith. People fear the senseless like-mindedness religion can inspire, and many are reluctant to put great faith in an unseen power, especially in an age of total information.

As modern commentaries criticizing religion arose, artistic works kept pace with them. The writings of famous author Stephen King are one such example. In the introduction to an essay on symbolism in King's *'Salem's Lot*, Leonard Mustazza, Ph.D., references King's non-fiction collection of essays, *Danse Macabre*. King writes "the tale of horror, no matter how primitive, is allegorical by its very nature" and Mustazza adds to that statement, writing "his (King) own brand of allegory often involves religion in one way or another" (Mustazza, 1994, p. 107). Many of King's other writings, including *The Stand, Carrie, The Mist,* and *Pet Sematary*, often incorporate religion.

The Role of God in Stephen King's *Desperation*

However, there is no Stephen King work that investigates religion quite as directly and with as much depth as *Desperation*, the novel that will be the focus of this essay. Whereas in other novels or stories, one will find some break from religious themes, *Desperation* presents no such reprieve. In the novel, God presents himself in a very direct manner. He speaks directly to characters and is the source of a multitude of miracles. However, despite his many benevolent acts, there is also the suspicion that God's blessings are perhaps curses in disguise, creating a conflict between God's compassion and God's cruelty. This essay aims to investigate the vital role religion plays in *Desperation*, and to discover what greater meaning King intends to convey. Furthermore, it aims to investigate God's exhibition of both cruelty and love, and to conclude which of these characteristics reigns most prevalent.

Investigation

Desperation is the story of a small desert mining town of the same name. It lies on Highway 50 in the state of Nevada, and has had its entire population massacred by the demon-possessed sheriff, Collie Entragian. The opening section of the story involves Entragian arresting a multitude of travelers that are traversing the highway. He falsely imprisons them all in the Desperation Town Jail. The captives escape the jail and dub themselves the Collie Entragian Survivor Society, which consists of the Carver family (notably including the pious 12-year-old David Carver), an engaged couple, a local veterinarian, and an aging writer and his roadie. Entragian's demon, Tak, begins a quest to kill all of them, but the group has a divine protection that allows them to turn the tables and destroy Tak itself, albeit with significant casualties. Notably, David's entire family is killed, leaving him bitter and angry with God for allowing such carnage.

Throughout the entirety of the story, God is a constant presence. He is consistently influencing the events that transpire, whether it is an obvious case or not. There exists the persistent question throughout the book, particularly in the latter part of the story, regarding God's true intentions. Two phrases, commonly repeated in the book, come to mind: "God is cruel" and "God is love". The two are in direct contention with one another, and there is a constant back-and-forth struggle between them.

There are many examples of God's cruelty in *Desperation*, each making a strong case for the denouncement of the deity. The first is the case of Brian Ross, David Carver's best friend from his hometown in Ohio. Brian was struck by a drunk driver, rendering him comatose. The driver could not remember committing the crime. David, against the advisory of his parents, visited Brian in his comatose state to find his best friend lifeless and the Ross parents in a state of extreme distress. In a hysterical rant, Mrs. Ross introduces to the reader the idea of a cruel God. She questions, "How could God be so merciful to someone who deserves to wake up screaming with memories of the blood coming out of my son's poor hurt head every night for the rest of his life?" and subsequently answers herself by saying, "The kind that wants that man to get loaded and do it again, that's who! A God who loves drunks and hates little boys!" (King, 1996, p. 168-170). This is a clear demonstration of the cruelty of God, a prime example of the timeless question: "Why do bad things happen to good people?" King ensures that

The Role of God in Stephen King's *Desperation*

Brian's mother specifically mentions God, drawing the reader's attention to God as the direct source of this injustice. The 1912 editorial from *The Biblical World* predates *Desperation* by over eighty years, but presents the same questions that King does in this scene, namely how could a God-figure permit such cruelty? It is interesting to note that Mrs. Ross's first inclination is to question why God isn't crueler. Her immediate instinct is that God should be more punishing of this man; that mercy is a ridiculous notion. This shows an imbedded belief in God's cruelty. Something, perhaps her upbringing or simply the modern American culture, has driven her to assume that God is usually without mercy. This matches the contemporary trend of the condemnation of religion. There is an expectation that God defaults to cruelty and is less disposed to mercy. Surely one could point to self-serving bias in this case, but when one considers Mrs. Ross's answer to her own question, it seems likely that she intends to condemn God's general favoritism as opposed to referencing this single case.

Theologian George Berry (1901) notes that God often manifests "not justice…but favoritism" as seen in His decision to destroy the Canaanites so that the Hebrews could obtain their land (p. 274). God takes action against the Canaanites because he prefers the Hebrews. "Lov[ing] drunks and hat[ing] little boys" is an allusion to the cruel favoritism that God is known for among Christian scholars; however, Brian's situation is more extreme than the case of the Canaanites, in which there was at least some defense for God's preference. The Canaanites, as Berry writes, were said to have "terrible moral corruption" (p. 274). In this case, God's actions can be justified, although his intervention still may seem unfair. Inversely, the God of *Desperation* has no moral reason to prioritize the drunk man over the young boy; it's an immoral favoritism. One should note that this is the first significant reference to religion in *Desperation*, but more meaningfully, it is the primary negative portrayal of religion in the first segment of the book, while the other acts of God in this opening segment initially seem to be acts of benevolence. This imbalanced ratio dilutes the significance of Mrs. Ross's damnations of God, as most of the other divine events surrounding it are viewed as positive.

Later, David confronts his religious tutor, Reverend Martin, regarding the cruel and unforgiving nature of God. Reverend Martin counters by admitting God can be cruel, but He is also forgiving due to how demanding He is. The Reverend thinks very highly of David, and sees him as a true convert. He is trying to nurture a love for God in David, as demonstrated by his insistence on instructing him, even in the face of his wife's discontent. He believes "that David Carver had been touched by God, and that God's touch might not yet have departed" (King, 1996, p. 186). Furthermore, he states that he enjoys the process of teaching the boy. Still, despite his deep desire to help David learn to love God, Martin admits that God is cruel; he relents that God is harsh. For Martin to so readily admit this shows that His cruelty is an essential part in the understanding of God. Martin is unable to tutor David regarding the love of God without first conceding that He is indeed a cruel being. Such an admission contrasts with Reverend Martin's caring and concerned nature, which only serves to increase the significance of his admission. If he didn't believe that teaching his pupil about God's cruelty was necessary, then he would've left it out in order to keep his teachings positive.

The Role of God in Stephen King's *Desperation*

Another discussion concerning God's cruelty is brought about by the demon Tak. At this point in the story, David's younger sister has been murdered by the possessed sheriff. Tak asks David, "Why would you pray to a God who kills baby sisters?" (King, 1996, p. 188). The demon is pointing out God's cruelty in an obvious attempt to waver David's faith. David easily dismisses this voice, which prompts the reader to do the same. It doesn't disturb David at all, which indicates how strong his trust in God is at this point of the story. The trust that David shows in God prompts the readers to place a similar faith in Him. So, even though David will later be tormented by the idea that his God allowed his sister to be murdered, the very same thought does little at that moment to tarnish his faith. This example of cruelty, unlike the others, actually improves the reader's view of God, due to how easily David's faith trumps Tak's words.

These examples of God's cruelty are diluted among the numerous positive portrayals of God and the several miracles performed by Him. They don't have a tremendous impact on the reader because they are merely a handful of negative examples among a sea of altruisms. In reality, their main significance is to foreshadow God's cruelty, as later seen in the novel.

While there exists a small amount of concrete examples outlining an immoral tendency in God, the amount of incidents in which God seems to play a positive role outnumber them greatly. For the majority of the book, it appears as if God is the Collie Entragian Survivor Society's greatest ally. However, toward the conclusion of the book, the characters realize that the miracles they have received could actually be clever forms of manipulation. A deeper inspection of these beneficial events reveals the possibility of a sinister, selfish motive within each.

The first miracle is the resurrection of Brian Ross, David Carver's young friend who was put into a coma by a drunk driver. At a time when everyone else had given up on Brian's chances of survival, "something whispered" to David that Brian was still alive (King, 1996, p. 170). This voice filled David with hope and guided him to the "Viet Cong Lookout" treehouse he and Brian had built when they were younger. Upon reaching the tree house, David questions why he's even come there, asks what force drove him there. Eventually, a voice replies, revealing itself as the voice of God, and tells David to pray for the health of his friend. David complies, saying, "God, make him better. If you do, I'll do something for you" (King, 1996, p. 178). He then leaves his Excused Early Pass from school in the tree fort, as an IOU for a favor to God (this favor, David later realizes, is to destroy Tak). God delivers on his promise, and miraculously revives Brian. The initial reader reaction to this miracle is to praise God for saving the boy's life. All notions of His cruelty previously mentioned by Mrs. Ross now seem irrelevant. David, despite being witness to Mrs. Ross's condemnation of God, quickly turns to religion after this experience. This shows that in the innocent, young mind of David, this miracle serves to redeem God, even after being exposed to Mrs. Ross's tirade. David's sudden and unexpected embracement of religion prompts the reader to follow suit and place their own trust in the God of *Desperation*. Initially, the resurrection of Brian Ross seems to be an act of mercy that sways the reader to view God as a protagonist along with David and the rest of the survivors. However, later in the book, David realizes the sinister nature

The Role of God in Stephen King's *Desperation*

of his deal with God, commenting, "The bad thing isn't that God would put me in a position where I'd owe him a favor, but that he'd hurt Brian to do it" (King, 1996, p. 621). The child recognizes God's cruel tendencies, and even accepts them to a certain extent. He realizes that he played pawn and puppet to God, yet has no issue with the fact that God has led him to Desperation to kill some powerful, ancient beast. The part that David takes issue with is the involvement of his friend, Brian, and that God chose to hurt someone in order to gain this favor. This is a child beginning his transcendence into adulthood, and for perhaps the first time, he is confronted with the evil manipulation that exists in the world and, in this case, beyond the physical realm. This is a pivotal stage of characterization for David, as it is his first true disapproval of God. Before this his only negative words concerning God were brief and unpassionate, and he proclaimed the cruelty of God with little conviction. Only now, after having witnessed a demonic massacre, is he able to castigate God with any confidence behind his words. The destruction and resurrection of Brian Ross can be independently viewed as acts of injustice and mercy, respectively, but when one considers the two events together in conjunction with the rest of *Desperation*, one is able to see that there is something more sinister at hand; one is able to recognize the manipulation that is taking place.

God's puppeteering of the Collie Entragian Survivor Society extends beyond Brian Ross's situation. God supplements them with a variety of miracles, most of which revolve around David, such as him being able to slip through the space between prison bars far too narrow for his body, dodging and killing an attacking coyote, being able to receive a signal with the same phone that others had tried with no reception, fabricating additional cans of food from nothing, and disrupting Tak's innate ability to track the group. In each of these examples, David is seen as the source of the miraculous events. These anomalous events cause the group to begin to side with David's religious ways, where initially they had dismissed his notions of God's role in what was happening. Some, such as Billingsley, the local veterinarian, go as far as to recognize God's blessings of David as necessary to their survival, commenting, "You're...special, the way you are. We need you, son" (King, 1996, p. 416). The other characters grow to become reliant on the child for guidance and assistance, and because of God's blessings upon David, they view him as a leader. One would typically find no evil in this, as God is assisting them in their survival, however the creation of a reliance on David does indeed have sinister implications. David is the only one who will do whatever God asks of him, as he is indebted by his favor to God. By bestowing these miracles upon David, God indirectly causes the other characters to depend on the boy, and therefore they will follow his lead. To be more precise, they will follow him in his quest to eliminate the demon, Tak. All these blessings are simply incentives for the entire Collie Entragian Survivor Society to join David in the crusade God has sent him on. Even these miracles, which, on the surface, seem to be beneficial in every way, have insidious consequences.

Another notable incident is the transformation of Johnny Marinville. Where Johnny was once cynical, depressed, and hopeless, he becomes a new man, all a direct result of a conversation Johnny has with David, which ends with him turning to God for salvation. The chapter ends, and the next time the

The Role of God in Stephen King's *Desperation*

reader sees Johnny, he is a new man. However, Johnny soon undertakes a suicide mission to blow up the resting place of Tak, killing himself and the demon, and fulfilling the mission God originally sent David to complete. There is a parallel here to David's original situation, an immediate miracle in exchange for an IOU. In Johnny's case, God saved Johnny from himself, and then redeemed the favor mere hours later, demanding Johnny's life. While God does rescue Johnny from his state of desolation, He doesn't allow Johnny to experience or enjoy his new life. It seems as if God only gives Johnny this second chance in order to use him to finish off Tak. His blessing is a cruel manipulation, and Johnny serves as nothing more than a means to an end.

Perhaps the most disturbing of the discoveries made in *Desperation* is that Johnny's favorite bar from his days in the Vietnam War and David and Brian's tree house both share the same name: "The Viet Cong Lookout." This sharing of names symbolizes the omnipotence of God, and is an allusion to the Lutheran ideals of predestination. It demonstrates that the God King portrays in *Desperation* has known of this meeting between Johnny and David for years. The two have been intricately connected since before David was even born. More to the point, God has known about the mass murders Collie Entragian would one day commit under the influence of Tak, He's known that David's entire family would die in such a horrible fashion, and He's been plotting to manipulate David for longer than David's actually been alive. Surely such a powerful God could've avoided all of this, He could've indeed saved them all, so why didn't He? It appears that God needed these innocent souls to destroy Tak, perhaps they were necessary sacrifices God had to make in order to prevent the demon from causing further harm. King raises the ethical question: Is it okay to manipulate an unwitting few in sacrifice for the greater good? The God of *Desperation* seems to believe so, as seen in His willingness to use the characters as nothing more than disposable tools. Perhaps His acts of cruelty are not of malicious origin, but rather born from necessity.

David, the most versed in Christianity of all the main characters, doesn't even begin to question God's motives or methods. He only ever challenges God's morals, but never why God does what he does. In a description of Tak, David deems him far beyond human understanding, and one can conjecture that he thinks the same of God, who is much more mysterious than Tak, as Tak has a conscientious thought process similar to that of a human. So, the answer as to why God didn't take a different course of action is unknown and cannot even begin to be understood. David is aware of this truth, so he simply says, "God is cruel," an unsatisfying and insufficient response. "God is cruel" does not offer any defense for God's actions, it is merely a statement of His nature, and David seems to be wholly content with this justification for a time. However, when his last surviving family member, his father, dies, David is no longer able to simply accept the brutality of God; no longer able to just say "God is cruel." Only after his father is killed, when he has nothing left, does David actually begin to question God's actions and morals.

One would think that such experiences would leave these characters bitter and angry with the God that had betrayed them once they realized the reality of their situation. However, that is not how King chooses to conclude the novel. Instead, as the final survivors drive away from the ruins of Desperation, David finds a note in his pocket that Johnny had slipped in earlier. It is the Excused Early Pass, David's IOU to God. On it, Johnny wrote "I John 4/8 Remember!" which David knows to mean, "God is love" (King, 1996, p. 692). David then begins to pray, as the book ends. One can hypothesize that David's return to God is his recognition of God's omnipotence and knowledge. David, prompted by the phrase "God is love," realizes that His actions may seem cruel, but they are perhaps for the greater good. David accepts his role as a puppet to a higher power because he has faith that his sacrifices are for a greater good. Additionally, King could've concluded his story at an earlier point, leaving both the reader and the characters filled with resentment toward God, due to his insidious ways, but he doesn't make that choice. Instead, King surprises the reader and ends the novel with a positive image of God. This can evoke several feelings from King's audience, including confusion, anger, joy, or pity depending on one's own experiences with religion. This moment of the proclamation of God's love isn't cathartic in the typical sense, as it is contradictory to what the rest of the story has reinforced. It is rather thought provoking, extending the audience's thoughts regarding religion past the final pages.

Conclusion

It is painfully clear that each of the miracles God grants upon the characters of *Desperation* employs a sinister component. Each blessing directly benefits God in His quest to destroy Tak, and even though these acts also seem to benefit the survivors, they only result in hurt. The Collie Entragian Survivor Society did not need to be so concerned about the possessed sheriff, but rather what grim fate they were being unwittingly driven to by a higher power. When all seemed to point to God as a malignant being, the conclusion of the book presents a clever twist on all that God has been built up to be, exerting a variety of emotions from readers. Overall, it seems that religion, in both fiction and reality, is a blessing and a curse, filled with mercy and cruelty alike. "God is cruel" just as often as "God is love."

For good or for bad, religion often makes people behave in ways that defy common sense. In *Desperation*, the portrayal of religion is extremely direct; it features a clear higher power that directly influences the real world. Religion's primary role in *Desperation* is to showcase the manipulation that religion is capable of. It can drive people to sacrifice everything in the name of their God. However, religion in *Desperation* is not solely a negative factor. David's re-embracing of God in the final pages fogs any clear message. There is some indestructible redeeming quality of religion that causes David to believe in the love of God despite what he has experienced. King may intend this as a warning, a cautionary tale, portraying religion as an abusive addiction, which one cannot quit no matter the pain they experience. David, who despite all that he endured, is still unable to turn away from a corrupt ruler in what could be viewed as a cruel and unusual case of Stockholm syndrome. Or perhaps King simply intends to say that yes, religion is inexplicable. Just as God is a higher being, incapable of being understood by mankind, the things He often inspires people to do are just as incomprehensible.

One may wonder what value can be found in the analysis of a contemporary horror novel. Many would cite the literary classics of Shakespeare or modern philosophical commentaries

The Role of God in Stephen King's *Desperation*

as more worthy of one's time in comparison. Some would even go as far as to say that horror fiction is merely fodder for the entertainment of the masses with no greater meaning in store for the trained reader. This paper refutes any such statement. King's religion-centric *Desperation* is capable of instilling the reader with moments of sheer terror, and yet it also provides the reader with the opportunity to discover greater meaning within the text. Additionally, one is never more vulnerable than when they are frightened, and this state of emotion allows them to unwittingly be more open to any new ideas garnered from the reading. A horror novel is perhaps more capable of prompting deep thought than any other genre, solely because of how pure and distressing the feeling of fear can be.

References

Berry, G. (1901). The Old Testament Teaching concerning God. *The American Journal of Theology, 5*(2), 254-278. Retrieved from **http://www.jstor.org/stable/3152400**

King, S. (1974). *Carrie*. New York: Doubleday.

King, S. (1980). *The Mist*. New York: Viking.

King, S. (1983). *Pet Sematary*. New York: Doubleday.

King, S. (1990). *The Stand*. New York: Doubleday.

King, S. (1996). *Desperation*. New York: Viking.

Mustazza, L. (1994). The Power of Symbols and the Failure of Virtue: Catholicism in Stephen King's "'Salem's Lot" *Journal of the Fantastic in the Arts, 3*(3/4 (11/12)), 107-119. Retrieved from **http://www.jstor.org/stable/43308202**

The Christian Conviction of the Greatness of God. (1912). *The Biblical World, 39*(6), 363-367. Retrieved from **http://www.jstor.org/stable/3141663**

From a Buick 8 by Stephen King: A Review

JACK KETCHUM

I took one look at the British cover art for *From a Buick 8*—a big old car in a shed, emanating jagged bolts of brilliant light—and thought, *uh-oh*.

Christine?

Could Stephen be repeating himself here?

It wasn't my favorite King book, tell the truth.

Then I read a chapter or so and thought of Emily Litella and smiled and said to myself, *never mind*.

Being a Manhattanite without much use for cars except that they're fun to drive now and then so long as you don't have to drive them *every* day, I have to go all the way back to my teenage years to even begin to understand the glamour of cars, and even then I come up short. I'm using the word "glamour" in the old sense now—the spell they cast, the enchantment. The deep personal hold they have on some folks. Why they'd rather be in *the car* than practically anywhere else in the world. Why they'd want to tinker with the car, test its speed and prowess on the turns and keep it squeaky clean, make sure the air in the tires is always *just so*. Back then I owned a big old Buick myself as coincidence would have it. Vintage '56, pink and grey. I thought it looked like something Elvis would want to drive before he struck it rich.

Since I was possibly the most ardent Elvis fan in all of Livingston, New Jersey, at the time I suppose that for me, that was enchantment enough.

But I doubt I ever kicked a tire in my life. Not even on the old Buick.

And here, in King's book, you have twenty years' worth of Pennsylvania State Troopers coming and going, some dying peacefully and others not so peacefully and some retiring and some just drifting away, all of them being replaced by new troopers and all of them *enchanted by the very same car*.

A 1954 8-cylinder Buick Roadmaster.

Two years older than mine and a hell of a lot more interesting.

King's story begins back in 1979 when this big old mint-condition midnight blue monster pulls up to the hi-test pump, one of only two at the little rural Jenny station, and a guy who looks like Boris Badinoff in *Rocky and Bullwinkle* gets out and tells Brad Roach—who is later to commit vehicular homicide—to fill 'er up, then heads toward the back, presumably to use the john. Never to be seen again.

After a while Brad calls the Troopers. He's afraid the owner might have dropped down the slippery embankment behind the station right down into Redfern Stream and drowned.

Besides, there's something *wrong* with this car.

It's rained the night before and the roads are a mess but there's not a drop of mud on the thing. It *sparkles*. The chrome sparkles, the windshield sparkles, even the goddamn paint

From a Buick 8 by Stephen King: A Review

sparkles. He's gone to fill 'er up as instructed and noticed that there's no license plate, not even a license plate holder and no inspection sticker, not a gum wrapper or cigarette pack or map on the floor, not so much as a smidgeon of dirt or sand. There's something funny about the dashboard too and there's no antenna for the radio. The steering wheel's so big it belongs on some rich guy's yacht.

Troop D officers Ennis Rafferty and Curt Wilcox take the call. Curt pops the hood for a look at the engine. He can't believe what he's seeing. The cylinders are all there but there's no distributor cap and no distributor and no generator and no alternator; there's nothing inside the radiator and no water and no antifreeze, and there's no fan belt, fan, or battery cables.

This is a car that can't run.

Half an hour ago it pulled up to the Jenny station and a fella who looked like a cartoon Russian spy got out and disappeared.

They haul it back to the shed at the station. And now *everybody* wants a look.

It goes on that way for twenty years.

Especially after the light shows. Lights that blind and fascinate.

Especially after Ennis Rafferty disappears from the shed one day.

Especially after the trunk starts *spewing things* that cannot possibly be alive yet *are* alive, at least briefly, misshapen monsters from god knows where and the interior begins *eating* things, living things, swallowing them up whole and sending them *off* to god knows where. And doing it selectively. Choosing.

This is one dangerous hunk of automobile. The boys of Troop D House are not only in its thrall. They're also its keepers. *Protect and serve.*

Ennis' partner, Curt Wilcox, is the trooper most affected by this glamour, this mystery, and over time becomes a student of the phenomenon, even going so far as to study anatomy so he can dissect the creatures the car's disgorged—trying to make some sense of it. It's not even a car, really. It's something else. So what is it? Where did it come from? Why's it here in the first place and to what end? The car baffles. It intrigues.

And every so often it does something awful.

Many years later, when Curt is cut down along the roadside by a drunken driver—that same Brad Roach who called the car in from the Jenny station—his young son Ned, adrift and bereft, starts hanging out with the guys of Troop D, doing odd jobs and eventually asking questions, trying to find some meaning in his father's seemingly senseless death and inevitably, just like his old man, trying to solve the puzzle of that midnight blue cherry Buick 8.

By then Troop D has pretty much adopted him. So one sunny afternoon they sit him down at the smoking bench outside the station to tell him the whole strange story.

• • •

"*There are Buicks everywhere*," says Sandy, the troop's top hat and the novel's principle narrator. The unexplainable's all around is what he's saying. And in his afterword King calls *Buick 8* "a meditation on the essentially indecipherable quality of life's events, and how impossible it is to find a coherent meaning in those events."

From a Buick 8 by Stephen King: A Review

True enough, as far as it goes. But his book's more about the search for meaning than the lack of it in the world, about how very human a thing it is to try to make sense of life and how fragile we are in pursuit of significance, about the nobility inherent in our struggle towards it—and all the risks, excitements and disappointments to be found along the way.

Buick's light years from *Christine*—in intent, emotional resonance and seriousness of purpose and design. This is mature, measured work gracefully written, more akin to *Hearts in Atlantis* or *The Green Mile* than to *Christine*. In fact there are striking similarities to *Green Mile*. What you've got here, basically, is a bunch of regular guys like the prison guards in *Mile*—plus one delightful sexy/motherly dispatcher named Shirley—who are trying to keep the lid on something far bigger than they are for the good of all, a community of flawed but benevolent souls who are in way over their heads with this one but trying to do the right thing according to their lights.

That their plan for containment and observation may very well go awry does not escape them. They proceed with it anyway.

And in the midst of great danger, almost foreseeable danger, for twenty years, life goes on.

• • •

There's almost a prescience here, I think. Just like there's almost a prescience to the fact that one of the book's lead characters is wiped away roadside in much the same fashion that the author himself damn near was, the summer after he wrote it. But King finished this novel in May of 2001, four months prior to September eleventh—when we in this country were visited by that same, almost foreseeable danger that much of the rest of the world has known for years. And what have we been doing since then—and what are we doing now—but *going on*?

That same eerie prescience extends to his central metaphor, the car.

Because what does the Buick do?

It obliterates, it swallows you up. It makes you disappear.

It delivers up deformed, unthinking monsters who are hostile to this environment, most of whom die upon contact with us folks. Monsters like living sacrifices from another world and another time.

Maybe it's just me. But maybe it was just in the air. Waiting, like the car, for its time.

•••

There's a tenderness and wistfulness about this book that you almost always find in Stephen's work to greater or lesser degree but which makes its presence felt quite strongly in the novels I've mentioned above as well as in pieces like "The Body," "Rita Hayworth and Shawshank Redemption," and *Bag of Bones*. That's not to say the shocks aren't there—you can bet they are—but they're balanced by a sense of easy familiarity and great sympathy with these people and their normal ongoing everyday lives, played out as they are against a backdrop of utter unknowable strangeness.

Think of chalk on a blackboard.

Our lives are the chalk. The strangeness is the blackboard. We can be erased, washed clean away—but the blackboard can't. Only shattered. And you wouldn't want

From a Buick 8 by Stephen King: A Review

to do that, would you? Otherwise the blackboard's just there, waiting naked for us to come make our mark, to inscribe it with our own brave stabs at meaning, as Stephen King does here.

Living in a Web of Mystery

BEV VINCENT

In a 2013 interview with Terry Gross on NPR's *Fresh Air*, Stephen King said that his mother used to read Erle Stanley Gardner and Agatha Christie novels when he was a kid. He found the Perry Mason books too stylish and artificial for his taste, but he loved Christie's mysteries. Everything was there in front of the reader, he said, so when Miss Marple gathered the suspects and pointed out details that should have been obvious to her from the beginning, King felt that they should have been obvious to him, too. However, he couldn't figure out how anybody could construct such detailed puzzles. "I was never built to be the sort of writer who plots things," he said. "I usually take a situation and go from there."

When he and his mother went into Lisbon Falls on their weekly grocery shopping trips, he would head straight to the drugstore, which had a couple of wire spinner racks stocked with hardboiled paperbacks featuring covers with scantily clad women. "She'd usually be dressed like a cigarette girl and there'd be a Lucky Strike hanging from one corner of her mouth and she'd have an automatic pistol in her hand," he told Gross. "The teaser line that I always loved the most was for a novel called *Liz*, where it said, 'She hit the gutter and bounced *lower*.'"

As a teenager, King submitted stories to *Alfred Hitchcock's Mystery Magazine* and *Ellery Queen's Mystery Magazine*, rarely garnering more than a form rejection. His first professional sale was to *Startling Mystery Stories*, although "The Glass Floor" is not a mystery.

A survey of his "best books of the year" lists from *Entertainment Weekly* reveals that King remains fond of crime fiction. Over the years, he has included novels by James Ellroy, Don Winslow, Laura Lippman, Stephen Dobyns, Gillian Flynn, Stieg Larsson, John Sanford, Lee Child, Joseph Wambaugh, Chelsea Cain, Kate Atkinson, Charlie Huston, George Pelecanos, Michael Connelly, Elmore Leonard, Robert B. Parker, Chuck Hogan, and John le Carré. His 2007 column spotlighting American author Meg Gardiner, who was being published in the UK but not in the US, raised her profile to the extent that she got a domestic publishing contract.

A discussion with Hank Wagner as he prepared an article for *Mystery Scene* in 2013 led to a list of King's novels and stories that might fall under the umbrella of crime fiction without too much of a stretch. His books often feature criminals of various stripes: embezzlers, thieves, rapists, stalkers, plagiarists, drug lords, child abusers, wife beaters and murderers. Some examples: Johnny Smith helps the Castle Rock police catch a serial killer in *The Dead Zone,* and the murder of two little girls is an inciting incident in *The Green Mile*, where just about everyone in Cell Block E was guilty of a major crime; *11/22/63* could be considered a mystery novel in which Jake Epping plays detective while trying to ascertain whether Oswald acted alone when he assassinated the president; Thad Beaumont in *The Dark Half* is a crime writer and nurse Annie Wilkes in *Misery* killed a number of her patients before kidnapping and torturing her favorite author; former LAPD lieutenant Jack Sawyer is asked to come out of retirement to assist local authorities in the Fisherman serial murder case in *Black House*; Dolores Claiborne explains why she killed her abusive husband in the novel of the same name.

In his essay in *Books to Die For: The World's Greatest Mystery Writers on the World's Greatest Mystery Novels*, Paul Cleve credited *Different Seasons* with convincing him to broaden his reading to include crime fiction, the genre in which he now writes. "Rita Hayworth and Shawshank Redemption" stands out in this collection as the story of a man falsely accused of murder who finds redemption while living for decades with hardened criminals, but "Apt Pupil" and "The Body" also have criminal elements.

Five years before King came up with the pseudonym Richard Bachman by combining Richard Stark (a pen name used by crime writer Donald Westlake) and Bachman Turner Overdrive, he published "The Fifth Quarter" under the name John Swithen (a minor character in *Carrie*). The story is a caper about dishonor among thieves, so it made sense that King would use a pen name to differentiate it from the horror tales he was publishing in men's magazines at the time. The first Bachman book, *Rage*, is about a school shooting and *Roadwork* might also be considered a crime novel, given the protagonist's actions.

A number of King's short stories involve gangsters and hit men. Robinson's wife in "Dolan's Cadillac" was murdered to prevent her from testifying against a crime lord. In "The Ledge," Stan Norris is forced to take an unusual walk by the mobster whose wife he's involved with. The mob gets into the stop smoking business—quite effectively—in "Quitter's Inc." "The Wedding Gig" is about a jazz band hired to play at the reception for a mobster's grotesquely obese daughter. The wife of a hit man's victim finds an innovative (albeit supernatural) way to repay him in "Battleground." Another hit man is given an unusual assignment in "The Cat from Hell." The uncollected story "Man with a Belly" is about a mobster who hires a hit man to rape his wife to punish her for gambling. "My Pretty Pony" is a flashback from an aborted novel about a boy who grew up to be a brutal hit man. King fictionalizes an incident from the John Dillinger saga in "The Death of Jack Hamilton."

Stories like "Strawberry Spring," "Cain Rose Up," "Suffer the Little Children," "The Gingerbread Girl," *Blockade Billy*, and "The Man Who Loved Flowers" feature serial killers and homicidal maniacs. A crime writer relies on his aggressive George Stark-like pseudonym to resolve a dangerous situation in "Rest Stop." In *On Writing*, King suggests that his story "The Night of the Tiger" was inspired by an episode of *The Fugitive*.

"The Doctor's Case," which first appeared in *The New Adventures of Sherlock Holmes*, is King's only published work that makes use of another author's characters, though it's not the only time he attempted to pick up where another crime writer left off (see below). In this story he gives Doctor Watson the opportunity to shine from the reader's perspective, as well as from that of Holmes.

"Umney's Last Case" is the closest King has come to date to penning a hardboiled crime story. It opens with a quote from one of the masters of noir, Raymond Chandler. It is the story of 1930s-era detective Clyde Umney, who discovers that his world is unraveling. Everyone he knows is leaving town or dying. Then he comes face to face with his creator, author Samuel Landry, who is remodeling Umney's universe prior to moving in. From Landry's perspective, Umney's life is ideal—an escape from the everyday horrors of the real world to a place where time never seems to pass.

Their conversation—a section called, appropriately enough, "An Interview with God"—is reminiscent of the meeting between Roland Deschain and Eddie Dean with their creator in the Dark Tower series. Umney is outraged at the suggestion that his existence is a work of fiction, but Landry asks him personal questions that he can't answer because Landry has never written them down. After Landry forces Umney to take his place in the 1990s, it doesn't take the former detective long to figure out how things work. He decides to write his own crime novel and set things right.

•••

In 1977, King moved to England with his family, intending to soak up enough local color to write a novel set there. One of the ideas he considered was a mystery set in the fictional universe of Dorothy L. Sayers—a Lord Peter Wimsey novel. He completed fifteen pages (one chapter plus the first page of a second), which he sent to his editor, Bill Thompson. It isn't known why he didn't finish it—whether Thompson didn't encourage him or he lost interest in it. The King family returned to the US after only a few months abroad.

In this manuscript, Wimsey is depressed because his beloved Harriet died during the German Blitz of London. The plot, as described by Stephen J. Spignesi in *The Lost Work of Stephen King*, is reminiscent of a British-era Hitchcock thriller, with someone sabotaging the brakes on Wimsey's car and a rural bridge he is known to use. Many years later, in *Bag of Bones*, Jo Noonan, who owns a complete set of Wimsey hardcovers, dubs the moose in Sara Laughs "Bunter," which is the name of Wimsey's faithful manservant.

King and crime writer John D. MacDonald were fans of each other's work. MacDonald wrote the introduction to *Night Shift* and his series detective, Travis McGee, was often seen reading a King novel. There had long been rumors of a "black" McGee novel (the books in the series all have colors in their titles) that would be published posthumously. However, this proved to be an urban legend. After MacDonald's death, King approached his son Maynard, asking permission to write a final McGee novel called *Chrome* to "put a button on the series," with the royalties from it going to charity, but he was turned down.

King's interest in writing crime fiction has been on an upswing of late. Three stories in *Full Dark, No Stars* are in that genre. "1922" is the confessional of a man who murdered his hectoring wife and dumped her body in the well because she wanted him to sell their farm and move into the city. The repercussions of this crime haunt him for the rest of his life. "Big Driver" is a revenge tale—a genre label that could be applied to some of the supernatural stories in *Creepshow*. A writer of cozy mysteries who is brutally assaulted takes matters into her own hands and punishes her attacker. She discovers that real life isn't as intricately plotted as fiction, so her plans don't work out as smoothly as she'd hoped, and she is fundamentally changed by her actions. "A Good Marriage," which uses the BTK killer as inspiration, is

Living in a Web of Mystery

about how someone might live for decades with a serial killer and never suspect—and what a person might do once they've stumbled upon the truth.

In 2005, when Charles Ardai asked King for a blurb to help promote his new noir imprint, Hard Case Crime, he did so knowing that King was fond of the genre. Instead of a blurb, King decided to write a book for them: *The Colorado Kid*. By King's own admission, the book wasn't a perfect fit. It's not noir, and the mystery of the man who shows up dead on the beach of one of Maine's many coastal islands (a setting that reminded King of the Christie novel *Ten Little Islands*) is unsolved. The two old men who run the island's newspaper regale their comely summer intern with the story. Though they warn her (and, by proxy, readers) that the mystery has no explanation, some people were frustrated by the open ending. The SyFy series *Haven* is a loose adaptation of *The Colorado Kid*, focusing more on supernatural mysteries than noir ones.

Several years later, King penned a whodunit for Hard Case Crime. Whereas King described *The Colorado Kid* as "bleu," *Joyland* is at least "gris" on the color scale. It is too cozy to be considered noir, where the world view is dour and pessimistic. The presence of a ghost and a young boy with precognitive powers is also not typical of the genre.

Joyland is a nostalgic coming of age novel about a lovelorn young man. The murder that took place at the carnival where Dev Jones works in 1973 turns out to be part of a series of crimes. He turns one of his friends into a reluctant detective, sending her to search for potentially related murders. He solves the crime and brings the killer to justice. King said he wanted the mystery aspect to feel organic instead of like a prefab creation. Although there is a trail leading to the solution, readers who identified the killer in advance were doing better than him, he said. "I got near the end of the book before I realized who it was."

He decided to release the book as a paperback original without the now customary ebook version. He wanted to recreate a retro experience that harkened back to the Mickey Spillane era. In his essay "Why Cling to the Past?" Charles Ardai, whose goal with Hard Case Crime was to give the impression that they had started publishing around 1945 and had never stopped, wrote, "[*Joyland*] is about memory; it's about the passage of time and its impact; it's about ways of life that existed once and are gone now, ones that deserve not to be forgotten. It's about all the things that led us to create Hard Case Crime in the first place."

•••

In early 2011, while he was driving from Florida to Maine, King stopped at a motel for the night and watched the news. One story was about a woman who had an altercation with another woman who was in line at a job fair. According to King, the woman in line had been caught sleeping with the other's husband. She eluded her attacker, but the other woman got into her car and drove it into the crowd, backing over more people on her way out. King decided that he wanted to write about the incident, although he didn't know at the time how he would do so.

For the next few months, he worked on the idea as he tried to get to sleep at night. He came up with what he thought would be a 12-page story about a man who deliberately drives his car into a crowd of people, killing several. The detective assigned to the case ultimately retires without solving the crime. The perpetrator writes the detective a boastful and taunting letter several months later, saying (in King's words), "I enjoyed the screams. I heard their bones breaking as this car went over them. I just absolutely adored the whole experience of killing all these people. The blood went up on the windshield, the headlights broke. I was wearing a mask so I knew they wouldn't know who I was. I didn't know if I'd get away with it...but I did. And it was great. And here's the thing. A lot of times guys like me, they do something like this and if the cops don't catch him right away, they say 'Well, wait. He'll try to do it again and then we'll catch him then.' But guess what? I don't want to do it again. Once was enough. I just relive the memories."

The killer's intention is for the cop to despair over his impotence and commit suicide, and that was how King intended to end the story. Instead he ended up with a 500-page manuscript for a hardboiled detective novel with no supernatural elements. King says *Mister Mercedes* has a lot to say on the subject of good and evil.

He first mentioned the book during a visit to UMass Lowell in late 2012. An interesting insight into the way he researches his books came to light during that appearance. While waiting to go onstage, King turned to Russ Dorr, his long-time research assistant, and asked him to find out something "for the Mercedes book." As reported in the university's alumni magazine, he asked how Ted Bundy was caught. "People do terrible things. And then do other things to get caught. Son of Sam, it was parking ticket. Ted Bundy, all I see is, 'routine traffic stop,' but I can't find the specific violation. Busted light?"

•••

In 2007, the Mystery Writers of America bestowed upon King their highest accolade: the Grand Master Award, which represents the pinnacle of achievement in the mystery field. Their press release referred to him as "the grand master of suspense" and said that he is "the natural successor to Edgar Allan Poe," the person for whom the MWA's annual awards are named (The Edgar Awards). Reed Farrel Coleman, Executive VP of the MWA, said, "King is that rare jack [of] all trades who masters all he attempts. He is a fearless writer."

Responding to the news, King said that he was delighted "to be joining the company of some of my greatest idols and teachers—people like John D. MacDonald, Ed McBain, and Donald E. Westlake. The award means a great deal to me personally, because it's an award from people who understand two things: the importance of good writing and the importance of telling stories." Other recipients of the honor include Alfred Hitchcock, Mickey Spillane, Raymond Chandler, Agatha Christie, and Mary Higgins Clark.

In an interview with *Parade* magazine prior to the release of *Joyland*, Ken Tucker commented that the book, although it contained supernatural elements, wasn't a horror novel. "I've been typed as a horror writer," King replied, "and I've always said to people, 'I don't care what you call me as long as the checks don't bounce and the family gets fed.' But I never saw myself that way. I just saw myself as a novelist."

So King is neither a horror writer nor a crime writer; rather, a writer exploring mysteries ranging from the mundane to the profound. He anticipated the criticism he would get for failing to explain how the Colorado Kid ended up dead on the beach. In the book's afterword, he says that he

Living in a Web of Mystery

could easily have come up with at least half a dozen solutions to the mystery, but that wasn't what interested him. The book was about the nature of mystery itself, not the resolution to one.

"I ask you to consider the fact that we live in a web of mystery, and have simply gotten so used to the fact that we have crossed out the word and replaced it with one we like better, that one being *reality*," he wrote. "It's the beauty of the mystery that allows us to live sane as we pilot our fragile bodies through this demolition derby world."

The One that Got Away

MICK GARRIS

You would think that getting a film or television adaptation based on a bestselling Stephen King novel off the ground would be an easy proposition. In fact, I know that most people do believe that to be the case, because whenever I'm at a film festival or convention or something, they all tell me that I should go make their favorite King projects with a proverbial snap of the fingers. Call up the studio or the network and make a deal and get to work.

Yeah, you might think that, but you would be wrong. That's not to say that some of these don't come together with the speed of a runaway train, but you'd be surprised by the patience and fortitude it can take to get even some of the maestro's most successful works off the ground.

It took over seven years of trying to get *Desperation* before the cameras, finally taking shape as a three-hour television event for ABC, though it was originally planned, and scripted by King, as a theatrical feature. The same happened with our most recent collaboration as of now, *Bag of Bones*. That one again began as a feature and ended up—five years later—as a two-part miniseries for A&E.

Even *Riding the Bullet*, which was based on one of the first ebook originals by a bestselling author, took years to get going, despite eager, excited agents, a spec script I was really proud of, and the blessing of the author himself. Planned as a studio feature, it ended up as a tiny indie that only got theatrical release in three cities, without a single television ad purchased to promote it.

But at least they got made, right?

The Stand was in development at Warner Brothers for fifteen years with George A. Romero attached to direct, and writers like Rospo Pallenberg toiling away before King took it over himself and wrote the 460-page screenplay that became such a massively successful miniseries (I never saw any but King's drafts, which was the most amazing script I'd yet read in my young life as a filmmaker). It was such a success that ABC gave King carte blanche to make the project of his choosing next for the network, resulting in *The Shining*... three years later.

After *The Stand*, Steven Spielberg, the first producer who had ever hired me as a screenwriter on *Amazing Stories* (I was the first writer hired to write a script for the show based on one of Spielberg's stories, before being hired on as story editor) was enthusiastic about collaborating with King and myself on a big-budget, big screen ghost story called *Rose Red*. Yes, the name is familiar to King-o-philes as it was made half-a-decade later as a miniseries for—you guessed it—ABC. When Spielberg was shooting *Hook* on the Sony lot (and Coppola was shooting *Bram Stoker's Dracula* there), I was shooting *Sleepwalkers* on adjoining stages. Steven visited my set to watch me work during the scene when Alice Krige makes the ailing cat-monster version of her son, played

The One That Got Away

by Brian Krause, rise from near death to dance with a terrified Mädchen Amick. Not that it wasn't an ordeal knowing Spielberg was sitting in the corner watching us work or anything. But the next day, he offered me another movie that never got made: a rendition of *Plastic Man*, which would have utilized the then-new process of CG morphing that I was using in that scene on *Sleepwalkers* and stretched it to its limits. Development hell, indeed.

But back to the King projects. This all ties together, right about now.

They took years, sometimes decades, but they got made and seen.

By now, Spielberg was eager for the three of us to follow up *The Stand* with something wonderful. It was not destined to be *Rose Red*, which fell apart, crashing and burning when not all creative minds met at the same bar.

But Steven (the one with the "v" is Spielberg; King's is with the "ph," but forever locked in my brain as "Steve") was a big King fan, and had wanted to work with him since *Poltergeist*, if not before.

For years, Spielberg and his production company, Amblin, have owned the rights to the King/Peter Straub collaborative novel, *The Talisman*. It's a masterwork of fantasy and horror, blending two genres that rarely work so well and in such a well-grounded literary planet. Steven had planned for years to bring it to the screen, for some time planning on directing it himself. I believe the first writer involved, and this was early in what was to become an incredibly illustrious career, was Richard LaGravenese, who, among other credits, wrote *The Fisher King* and *Water for Elephants*, as well as becoming a respected director, himself. He also wrote the original drafts for *Unbroken*, a film about my father-in-law, on which I am an Executive Producer.

Well, word was that they just couldn't get the script right for the movie, which is not surprising. The book is some 800 pages long, and we all know what happened with *The Stand* after gestating for fifteen years before being translated into an eight-hour extravaganza. And *The Talisman* was at least as complicated, and even more adventurous, filled with magical, richly imagined fantastical landscapes and creatures and huge effects scenes.

So...where did they turn? After years of feature development, Amblin made a deal with ABC to turn it into a two-part miniseries. And I was hired to adapt and direct this gargantuan undertaking.

I started out as a writer. From that age of twelve, I took writing very seriously, constantly writing fiction and eventually journalism and music and film evaluation and interviews. It was as a writer that Spielberg first hired me, and all involved were very excited at the prospect of making *The Talisman*—like *The Stand* before it—long enough to do the massive story justice.

I'm good friends with intimidation; I had gotten to know it well when that first 460-page *Stand* script landed on my doorstep, when the largest film I had directed previously was a little opus called *Critters 2*. I knew it when Spielberg called my home to ask me to come on board as story editor on *Amazing Stories*...this while I was briefly collecting food stamps. It had me hyperventilating when Steven asked me to come to his home to screen the incomplete *Sleepwalkers* for him and his wife, Kate Capshaw. And imagine the feeling of being handed the reins of the

The One That Got Away

Psycho legacy, directing Anthony Perkins in a prequel to *that* masterpiece.

Well, *The Talisman*, we all know, is beloved by millions, with the same rabid fierceness that most of the King books are embraced. So here were my walking orders: take a vast novel that spans time and place and dimensions, and turn it into four hours of spectacular cinematic television, something with scope and vision and magic and depth and emotion and everything else that comes with it. And with Spielberg, King, Straub, a studio, and a network looking over my shoulder.

Easy peasy, right?

So I took a paperback copy of the book and read it over three times, scribbling notes in the spaces, dog-earing pages, memorizing, really familiarizing myself with this magical world, immersing myself in the prose and the story that would be put on film. Adapting a beloved book is no easy task, and I've come in contact with more than a few haters who despise anything that might change turning fiction into cinema. Richard Matheson once told me something that has stuck in my brain in the decades since: books are internal and film is external. The twain—though they may get close enough to touch—can never really meet.

But great movies can be made from great books; it's been done before and it will be done again. They may be different media, but storytelling is what they are all about, and if you can summon up the emotions, the feelings, the touchstones of the prose and put it up on the screen, you are a graduate of the arts. You always have to leave something out or change it or combine it, and when you do, it's always somebody's favorite part...and that somebody will let you know about it.

You wear the hide of a rhinoceros when you turn books into film. Just sayin'.

And so I set to the task; I took my dog-eared, yellowing, broken-binding paperback and sat down at the computer and typed. And typed. And typed. I loved the experience, getting into these characters, really exploring and spelunking these invented worlds, telling the tale of a mother and a son, on earth as it is in heaven, and the profound relationship between a boy and his Wolf.

I swear that by the time I was ready to write, I could tell where King left off and Straub took over. It was that intimate an experience.

I write fairly quickly, maybe because I type well and lose myself in the process. But the material laid itself out so naturally, the prose in the book was so damned cinematic, that this was no chore. Working on an average of ten pages of screenplay a day, it wasn't long before I had a first draft of over two hundred pages. And I was excited by it. In many ways, I felt that the book that King and Straub had concocted opened a door to some of my best work as a screenwriter.

Fantasy is not usually my favorite form of the imaginative muse. But this fantasy was so grounded in a very real world and in such complex and sympathetic characters, even with giant Herbertian sandworms thrashing about the landscape, it all felt true and honest and human and compelling. I finished, I went over it, I read it again, reworked some of it, read it again, then, held my breath and turned it in. I would be directing as well, and was eager to find out the when and where of this magical production.

And my work was met with a deafening silence.

The One That Got Away

I had heard from some of the people at Amblin great, encouraging, enthusiastic words, but the network had nothing to say. Not a thing.

Okay, it can take a while to digest a 200-page script, I get that. But the weeks ticked by, my agent called the network and they just had nothing to say about anything.

The Talisman became the one that got away, it seemed.

Did they hate it? I can take it, just tell me, I thought. I've had projects crash and burn before—witness *Rose Red*, for God's sake—and I would be crushed, but I'd recover. I promise, I won't take it personally.

But it just died, and there was no funeral.

Then...there was news. ABC was at their nadir at the time; their new shows were dropping like Bay Bridge suicides and ratings were plummeting. The network was bleeding profits in outgoing gushes. Between the cost of King, Spielberg, Straub, producers Kathleen Kennedy and Frank Marshall, and, to a far lesser extent, myself, the network just couldn't afford such a massive project. And that was just the above-the-line talent! Forget the cast, which would cost a fortune, and the ability to tell this giant story itself, which would test the boundaries of special effects technology at the time, or even now, for that matter.

Nope. This one was dead at ABC.

But wait! A glimmer of hope!

Amblin had decided to go back to making it a feature again! This was exciting news that my agent delivered to me.

But there was a proviso. They loved the script, but they were bringing in a director who had just been nominated for an Academy Award for *House of Sand and Fog*, Vadim Perelman. Okay, I didn't have feature credits like that, and I could understand the upscale version the studio and Amblin wanted to make. But they loved the script. But it was a television script for a four-hour TV miniseries. And once they decided to go the big Hollywood feature film version, I was left choking on its dust. I heard less and less about it, and soon, that phone line went dead.

For another few years, new names would pop up in *Variety* of directors and screenwriters who were attached to make the movie, and it really seemed like it was going to happen. But those announcements came fewer and further between. So far as I can tell, they have ceased completely.

The time had come to move on with my life and my career, and, like the shark that can't remain still or it dies, I continue to swim.

The Talisman has slipped away. The script remains one of my favorite things I've ever written, and though I haven't looked at it in years, it still fills me with a feeling of accomplishment, regardless of that fact that it was never turned into a film. I can't say that I still have hope that it will one day reach the screen, but a guy can dream, can't he?

My Accidental Obsession with Stephen King

JAY FRANCO

This essay is dedicated to my father, Joseph James Franco [1943-2000], or simply, JF, as his friends called him.
He taught me so much. Miss you every day, pops.

I became a Stephen King fanatic sort of by accident. Well, not quite but perhaps more by circumstance. Let me tell you my story. I should start off by stating a truth: I grew up terrified of Stephen King and his stories. My love of reading began with comic books and fantasy novels, and eventually my love of superheroes and fantastic stories developed. I would often get caught in high school with a fantasy paperback hidden in my lap as I tried to pay attention in class. I was also the guy in the locker room reading *Daredevil* or the *Uncanny X-Men* before practice.

At home I lived in the shadow of my father's obsession with horror films—and the terrifying picture of Bela Lugosi he hung in the basement—as well as my older sister's budding addiction to horror novels. Stephen King was clearly destined to be part of my future; I just didn't quite know it yet.

My comics and fantasy reading laid the foundation for a love of reading in general which steered me to major in English Literature in college. This would lead me to a career working in book publishing. My first job was as a production assistant at a larger medical publisher, where I worked for almost 2 years. After that I landed a position as an Editorial Assistant for the Mystery Guild Book Club. I saw taking this position as a way to begin working directly with fiction, as I was not interested in continuing working with medical books and journals. I should also note that when I started at the Mystery Guild, Stephen King was not an author we sold; he was with Book-of-the-Month Club, a competitor at the time (some time later our companies merged). In other words, even though we had some terrific authors at the Mystery Guild, we didn't have Stephen King. Bummer.

At some point while working at the book clubs, something propelled me to pick up and read my first Stephen King novel. It was *'Salem's Lot*; I chose this novel specifically as at the time it was the Stephen King book that I had heard was really good but I somehow managed to not learn the details of the story. All I knew was that there was a vampire in it. And I didn't like vampires all that much. It was finally time to face my fears.

Even with horror films and television as a constant part of the background noise of my youth, I had also somehow missed the 1979 TV adaptation of *'Salem's Lot* starring David Soul as Ben Mears. And I'm not passing judgment on the adaptation—I've liked and disliked some other King adaptations—but I hadn't seen this one and I was glad to go into the book cold. My father's love of horror films along with my sister's reading made me appreciate King's work

My Accidental Obsession with Stephen King

in various forms long before I started reading him myself. But I did enter into this book with very little prior knowledge of the contents...isn't that the best way, anyway? And I read with trepidation little by little, creeping along until I reached the end. I was petrified.

Another Constant Reader was born.

I worked at the book clubs for several more years, and eventually became the graphic novels buyer for the Science Fiction Book Club—a detail which will prove significant some time later in my working on the Stephen King Library Desk Calendar as contributor and then later as Editor.

By 2006 I had worked my way up to full Editor. I was part of the team acquiring books for the Science Fiction Book Club and I began running and selecting books for the military history non-fiction club, Military Book Club. It was a well-balanced job if you ask me. Later that year, Marvel Comics announced plans to produce a series of Dark Tower comic book adaptations, and more importantly, that Stephen King was coming to New York to join the panel of Marvel creators to talk about it at the New York Comic Convention. I was asked to cover this panel, and write my first essay for the 2007 calendar for the Stephen King Library and Book-of-the-Month Club, who'd been creating the exclusive calendar for many years. This was my first step from being just a reader of Stephen King, to participating in a major discussion of his cultural impact.

After covering the Marvel Comics/Stephen King panel at New York Comic Con and writing my essay for the 2007 calendar, my newfound interest in King's work only grew and I had a lot more reading ahead of me.

Time continued to pass as I worked my way through most of King's legendary backlist and worked my way up to a Senior Editor at the clubs. After ten years in those halls, it had become time to move on. During the next phase of my career, a fruitful few years as a freelancer, a unique opportunity came to me. I was asked if I would like to be editor of the 2010 Stephen King Library Desk Calendar. It was early 2009 at the time; much of the calendar work is done months in advance as you can imagine, in order to allow time to create all of the content and then print and ship the calendar, much in the same way a regular book is put together.

I was honored, especially to follow in the footsteps of the most recent editor of the 2009 calendar, Robin Furth, of whom I was a big fan and well aware of her past working directly for King and of the terrific reference books she'd written about The Dark Tower series. I hoped she would continue to contribute an essay once I took over as Editor. She did and continues to contribute to this day.

It was also an opportunity for me to reach out to authors and other publishing professionals I knew—reach real die-hard King fanatics whom I admired—to see if they'd each be willing to write a few hundred word essay about the influence King's work had on them or to muse on a topic related to whatever theme I chose for the upcoming calendar.

I was to be the person responsible for selecting the theme for the calendar. That, in and of itself, was very cool as it allowed me to direct the creative flow of the content—the essays as well as the design approach to the cover and interior page design.

For those not familiar with the Stephen King Library desk calendar; it is a spiral-bound weekly calendar with an

My Accidental Obsession with Stephen King

essay for each two-page spread. The editor selects a theme and contacts writers to write approximate essays tied to the theme or perhaps cover a recent bit of news or write a random piece related to King's work. The editor also selects excerpts from King's novels and short stories to complement the other essays and the overall theme, and seeks permissions to use them in the calendar—pulling it all together within the timeframe that is allotted. The editor also puts together trivia tests and quizzes along with other King-related minutiae, for an end product that will appeal to any King fan, old or new.

Needless to say, I was ecstatic to be editor and get the opportunity to select the theme and get started on the project. I can still recall when the theme first came to me, as if whispered by twin girls in a dark hallway. *The Shining*, they said. Little did I know at that time that I would go on to edit and co-write the calendar for the next five years. Each time it was a challenge and each year it was rewarding for different reasons.

Between the impressive body of work that King has produced, the numerous film, television and comic book adaptations, and the ever-growing cultural icon he'd become, it seemed there was always a bit of news about King that I was able to tap into for essays for the calendar. I came to learn while working on this wonderful project that by hinting an upcoming theme to contributors—myself included—it inspired ideas to come screaming from the corners of the mind. It made for some fun reading, and I hoped the people who bought the calendar felt the same way.

The schedule was no joke, with only a few months to solicit all the material, edit, correspond with contributors, all the while working with the art director on developing the cover art concept, and pulling it all together—all while writing a lot of the content myself. It felt like running a small newspaper, and then when all the content was submitted and reviewed, once we double-checked and edited the page proofs and tried to catch anything that slipped by, then it was off to the printers, and that was like sending a kid off to college. Except this kid comes home in the fall, as that is when calendars for the following year aim to be in the warehouse to fulfill orders.

That is the process in a nutshell. I experienced it for the first time with the 2010 calendar, then went on to edit and co-write the calendar for an additional four years, leading up to now. Each year I've worked with a slightly different handful of essayists, all King enthusiasts, some professionally so, and others book professionals who've had a lot to say about King's work.

It has been a vicious cycle of becoming more obsessed with each newer work, such as *Under the Dome* and *11/22/63*, while at the same time trying to become even more familiar with the deep backlist, and keep all the threads straight in my head of course. As a few of my contemporaries will attest, King scholarship is an addiction. Reading him might start as a fling, or as a small byproduct of a love of books. I already have too many reading obsessions: comic books, fantasy novels, thrillers, historical fiction, World War II non-fiction, post-apocalyptic fiction—oh, I'm sure I'm forgetting a few, the list goes on and on.

And yet, here I am. Working full-time for the past few years in special sales for a prominent imprint at one of the big publishing houses, where I somehow still manage to find the time, almost always working well past the stroke of midnight,

My Accidental Obsession with Stephen King

on the calendar: drafting ideas, sending emails, saving notes (mostly digital now, but not all...I still love a good pen and a trusty notebook). Even I can clearly admit the worm has certainly turned when I'm the one emailing my sister to ask if she's checked out the newest Stephen King book, as I'm already elbow deep and falling further into madness.

And what I've come to learn while reading Stephen King: He's talking to all of us.

His stories appeal to everyone, not only horror fans. He writes about people, not only the horrible or amazing things that can happen to them. King writes about ordinary folks in extraordinary circumstances and how they react to situations under pressure. This is what makes his books so interesting, even more, this is what makes his characters so relatable—it's the flaws, all the weird, the strange ways people react to, say, evil, or a monster, or an invisible dome. Some embrace it, others eschew it...few transform into heroes and fight it. And sometimes "It" is the problem.

I didn't understand early on what it was all about. It was right there in front of me, but I was too naïve to see it. I eventually dove into the ice cold water, and have been swimming ever since. Each King story brings something new, characters I want to experience life with, and I know there are a lot of others out there like me. We are the Constant Readers, even though some have joined the pack a little later than others.

Stephen King Celebration

CLIVE BARKER

A speech delivered at the Canadian Booksellers Association Lifetime Achievement Award presentation to Stephen King, Toronto, 8 June 2007.

Good evening:

You're probably all familiar with the notion that appears in science-fiction films and TV shows about parallel universes. You know how the basic idea goes: a group of characters, journeying into the past, discover that they have made some error that changes the future. The roads divide. The future comes now in two distinct forms.

Indulge me for a moment, will you, and allow that such a strangeness is possible. In one of those futures this event is taking place, the same in every detail but for one: the seat from which I just rose is empty. Clive Barker is not a guest at this celebration. In fact, nobody here has ever even heard of him.

Why? Because I never had a career. I live in England, probably still in my home town, Liverpool. Maybe I am an English Teacher. Every now and then I think about the stories

I published 25 years ago and wonder about trying to write some more. But the moment has passed. In this future, Clive Barker will live out his days with hundreds of ideas in his head which he never committed to paper.

This other future—that empty chair—isn't so far-fetched an idea. When my English publishers put out my first stories, *The Books of Blood*, they were greeted with a very English silence. Polite and devastating. I don't know what I was expecting, but it certainly wasn't this smothering shrug.

And then, a voice. Not just any voice. The voice of Stephen King, who had made people all around the world fall in love with having the shit scared out of them. He said, God bless him, that I was the future of horror. Me! An unknown author of some books of short stories that nobody was buying. Suddenly, there is a phantom present in that chair.

Stephen had no reason to say what he said, except pure generosity of spirit. The same generosity he has shown over the years to many authors. A few words from Stephen, and lives are changed forever.

Mine was. I felt a wonderful burden laid upon my shoulders; I had been *seen*, and called by name, and my life would never be the same again.

So, may I take this opportunity to thank the man we celebrate here tonight; on my own behalf, certainly, and on behalf of all the other authors whose futures have been transformed by him? I have a chair here because of Stephen, and an audience whose first introduction to my works was brought about because Stephen had recommended me to his immense audience.

Now I do my best to be a voice for others. To pass the parcel along. As a writer, Stephen has taught me countless lessons in storytelling. But it is the lesson of how to *give* that echoes most powerfully through my life. And will, I hope, echo on through the lives of others as I support the next generation of writers with my own sincere enthusiasm.

Thank you for the chair, Stephen.

From the bottom of my heart, thank you for the chair.

CEMETERY DANCE PUBLICATIONS

We hope you enjoyed your
Cemetery Dance Paperback!
Share pictures of them online, and tag us!

Instagram: @cemeterydancepub
Twitter: @CemeteryEbook
TikTok: @cemeterydancepub
www.facebook.com/CDebookpaperbacks

Use the following tags!

#horrorbook #horror #horrorbooks
#bookstagram #horrorbookstagram
#horrorpaperbacks #horrorreads
#bookstagrammer #horrorcommunity
#cemeterydancepublications

SHARE THE HORROR!

Book Ad to come

HORROR DNA

MOVIES
COMIC BOOKS
MUSIC
BOOKS
VIDEO GAMES

IT'S IN OUR BLOOD
horrordna.com

www.ingramcontent.com/pod-product-compliance
Lightning Source LLC
LaVergne TN
LVHW041541070426
835507LV00011B/866